THE BEACON LEADERSHIP TECHNIQUE

THE BOOK ON BUILDING EFFECTIVE RELATIONSHIPS FOR HIGH-FLYING EXECUTIVES

NESLYN WATSON-DRUÉE
& RAYMOND AARON

ISBN:9781928155485

PUBLISHED BY:
10-10-10 PUBLISHING
MARKHAM, ON
CANADA

Contents

Foreword

Climbing the corporate ladder means becoming more astute about business and financial management, but it doesn't necessarily make you a great leader. The qualities of a great leader come from within. Leadership requires a healthy mindset that comes from understanding and overcoming any negative conscious and unconscious behaviors that affect the way in which you interact with others.

A number of factors determine the way you act, only some of which you are aware consciously. Many of them arise in childhood, where you first exhibit behaviors that may later hold you back as reactions to the way you were treated by others, especially the significant adults in your life. Experts refer to these associated feelings and behaviors as your 'inner child.'

Letting go of those old reactions is essential if you are to develop a healthy relationship with yourself, which is the first step in developing superior leadership skills. No executive, whether they have risen through the ranks of a corporation or built a company through entrepreneurial efforts, can manage or command for success without cultivating the behaviors and qualities of a great leader. Perhaps no one understands this better than Dr. Neslyn Watson-Druée and Raymond Aaron. In this book, they show you how to address the inner-child issues that are holding you back. You will also learn how to develop emotional intelligence and establish an inner clarity that, when combined with your business acumen, will help you become the great leader you are meant to be. The authors, both exceptional and renowned business coaches, are especially adept in helping people identify and achieve both business and personal goals. They lay out a clear path towards establishing a great leadership style that can be implemented as the standard for interaction at every level within your organisation.

The journey you are about to embark on with Druée and Aaron will change your entire life for the better. By following the powerful steps outlined in this book, you will experience benefits that go far beyond your business relationships. By eliminating negative behaviors and attaining peace with your past, you will also experience a new sense of joy in your personal life. The same qualities you will be able to bring to leading the people you manage will also help you build better, stronger and healthier relationships with everyone who is important to you.

This is an incredibly powerful and important book for everyone who wants to improve the ways in which they interact with others, especially those who wish to command a business team towards superior results. Be prepared to open yourself up to new opportunities to lead, grow and experience an inner happiness that will bring you greater success in all aspects of your life.

Nik Halik,
Bestselling author and Founder and CEO of Financial Freedom Institute, Money Masters Global, The Thrillionaires® and iCoach Global

Recommendations

Everything in life is a function of right relationship and impeccable integrity and Neslyn is the Master of the subject. Let Neslyn.com lead you as a Master to full participation inside WisdomWorldWide.com, participating on the wall, the calls and the ball.

Dr Jack King
Author of THEhealingINNERnet.com

Recommended reading if you're looking to create a shift in your life and in the world. In this book Neslyn highlights something that anyone in business and life eventually realizes and that is the importance of people working on themselves to get to know themselves so that they can learn to respond to all that happens and create the successes they need to. The book is clearly written and will be an easy read that will serve those to new the concepts as well as the busy entrepreneur, CEO or Manager. Even if you've done the work on yourself already, this book can serve as a useful tool for others you work and interact with to help make real win/wins for all as they go through their journey - either privately or in groups.

Simon Hedley
The Strategic Alchemist

Introduction

Welcome to *The Beacon Leadership Technique: The Book on Building Effective Relationships for High Flying Executives.* Within these pages, Raymond and I present the essence of the insights arrived at through my explorations of both theoretical and applied relationship management. While the emphasis is on organisations, we take the view that healthy organisations depend to a large extent on healthy individuals, and that it is the executive's responsibility to create a container in which productive relationships can blossom.

As an executive or business owner, it is therefore your role to set the standard for interaction at every level within your organisation. However, you cannot do this effectively until you commit to bringing into balance the one crucial relationship that all others depend on: *your relationship with yourself.* It all begins inside, and you need tools to help you change your inner vibrations, and thus your point of attraction. To that end, we begin our discussion with an exploration of how to heal your subconscious *inner child* aspect, in order to reclaim your power and authority from stored memories of childhood traumas large and small. This is some of the most empowering work you can do to increase your confidence and effectiveness in all types of relationships.

Once you have built a strong internal foundation through inner child work, you're ready to leverage the power of *emotional intelligence* to build relationship capital both within your organisation and beyond it. This is the key to firmly establishing all your business relationships on the core transformational leadership values of equality, mutuality, and empowerment.

The tools presented in the first two chapters are designed to help you become conscious of previously unconscious thoughts and beliefs, creating space for you to establish *clarity*. In Chapter 3, we discuss why inner clarity is crucial to maintain at every moment. Our external reality reflects our internal reality, and getting clear about why you have the aspirations, desires, and passions that you do activates the law of attraction to bring you the results you most desire. In Chapter 3, you will find out how to get clear and stay that way.

Healing the inner child, developing emotional intelligence, and establishing inner clarity gives you a solid internal foundation from which to respond to the conflicts and negotiations that are an inevitable part of business, and management in particular. We give these subjects a thorough treatment in Chapters 4 and 5, illuminating the ways in which conflict in relationships can act as a catalyst for growth at both the individual and collective level. We place emphasis on not viewing conflict as indicative of a leadership failure on your part, but instead to regard it as a normal aspect of human relationships.

Our focus in Chapter 6 is on how you can get what you want by giving those you lead aspects of what they want as well; that is, how to live in a world of win-wins. We share what I have learned about how living in integrity with your values boosts your ability to achieve greater-than-imagined results. We also speak to the way that self-limiting beliefs can stop you from reaching your goals, and how to let them go.

After emphasizing transformation through personal growth, we remind you in Chapter 7 that Ralph Waldo Emerson was right when he said that 'life is a journey, not a destination.' When you strive to make your relationships enjoyable, you will reach your goals with less effort and greater fulfilment. In Chapter 8, this theme continues with a reminder that life is about learning, and when you bring this understanding to your relationships, you improve your ability to see yourself, others, and the world around you for what they are. You begin to understand that there will always be more to learn, and learning can be *fun*. Revolutionary stuff for many leaders!

We conclude with a discussion on how all these elements synthesise to help you lead more competently, efficiently, and joyfully. That's why we wrote this book after all: to help you leverage the power of relationship to create positive synergy in every aspect of your business.

Dr. Neslyn Watson-Druée, CBE and Raymond Aaron

Chapter 1
Relationship with Yourself

"What lies behind us and what lies before us are tiny matters compared to what lies within us."
— *Ralph Waldo Emerson*

Most of us have been told that 'our greatness lies within' by one or more teachers. However, our understanding of this idea may have remained superficial, if we were not given tools to uncover that greatness. In my own work and in the work I have done with Raymond Aaron, I have learned that **the first step to becoming a master of all relationships is to master your relationship with yourself, and that one of the best ways to do this is to heal your inner child.** When you work with your inner child, you are acknowledging and accepting every element of your being, which is the first step that must be taken before transformation can occur. In this way, you can bring to light patterns and feelings that have been hidden in the shadows of your subconscious mind since childhood.

I believe that listening to the voice of the inner child unlocks the deeper architecture of our multi-dimensional sense of self. As you reinvent yourself at each stage of life, you assign new descriptions for your inner protector, warrior, sage, magical child, innovator, and so on. **I believe**

that we are spiritual beings having a human experience, and that your journey with your inner child can open up new dimensions for your transformation and growth.

Nurture and Connect With Your Inner Child

Where do we begin the process of healing our inner child? We must start with an understanding of how the emotional, or limbic, brain works. Your emotional brain holds the key to all your relationships, and the reasons for this are twofold; first, it is responsible for the activation of all the emotions that get triggered by relationships, and second, it controls the processes of memory. Your emotional brain is the repository of all that has ever happened to you, and is largely responsible for creating the views of life that you formulate from your experiences. It is the part of the brain that is responsible for recording your earliest memories of relationship, as well as for learning in other areas during the first three years of life. For this reason, healing your inner child is one of the most effective ways to re-program your emotional patterns.

The emotional brain includes a structure called the amygdala, which plays a key role in the processing of emotions. In early childhood, the activity of the amygdala takes place beneath your conscious awareness, but it plays a crucial role in shaping your patterns of response to interactions and situations. For many of us, our earliest conscious memories begin around the age of three because, prior to this, our subconscious emotional brains were very much in the driver's seat.

From Childhood To Business

Why is this relevant for business and management? The answer lies in the fact that your childhood experiences, as well as learning to emotionally navigate different types of relationships as a child, determine the patterns of response that you will exhibit in such relationships for the rest of your life. For example, the way that the adults charged with your care interacted with you when you were vulnerable creates the mould from which all your subsequent authority relationships are cast.

The responses of our caregivers to our demands for love and attention can cause us to form unconscious defence mechanisms that are deeply entrenched in the limbic brain. While these may enhance our ability to survive as children, they often hold us back from full self-expression and empowerment in relationship when we reach adulthood.

There are a number of such mechanisms that commonly form as a result of typical adult responses to the challenges of caring for young children. Some examples include closing off emotionally, making trouble to get attention, and avoiding any and all conflict due to fear of anger or rejection. As anyone who has raised children knows, in those early years it is all too easy to lose your patience or get drawn into a battle of wills with the young child. Rare is the parent who has the presence of mind to respond consistently with calm and clarity to the child's demands, with an awareness of what is really going on at a subtle level.

Generally, the ones who are able to do this have one of two things going for them: either they made working on themselves a major priority before having children, or they were one of the fortunate few whose parents had done so themselves. For the rest of us, it's no use blaming our parents; like everyone, they were just doing the best they could with what they had at the time. The good news is that recent breakthroughs in neuroscience have validated the experience of many people that it is possible to consciously re-shape these subconscious emotional programs, so they work *for you*, rather than against you. As a coach and therapist, it's been my experience that inner child work is one of the most effective ways to do this.

Dr. Allan Schore is a pioneer in integrating social, biological, and psychological theory. He explains in his written works that a toddler's emotional state at approximately two years of age largely determines whether or not key connections within the brain are established and used. He describes how the brain's connectivity is determined by the quality of care a child receives at this time, and how this connectivity shapes the child's developing worldview, mindset, sense of self, impulse control and ability to relate to others.

These early years matter a great deal, because your relationship with yourself is mediated by your inner child. From your first breath to adolescence, the beliefs that you take on in your formative years filter your perceptions and determine your internal and external responses. That is why it is important to review your beliefs and take steps to clear out the ones that no longer serve you. If you don't make a conscious effort to shine light on these unconscious beliefs, they can and will sabotage your best efforts to create the life experiences you want.

Why Healing Your Inner Child is Pivotal

I believe that, just as you sought love and attention from your caregivers as a young child, your inner child, who is a psychological vestige from this time, continually seeks these same things from your adult self. It just may be that:

- You neither understand the importance of communicating with your inner child, nor the benefits of healing past traumas that may still be affecting him or her.
- You are unaware that success or failure in all your endeavours is strongly influenced by your inner child.
- You have never experienced or been taught how to connect with your inner child.

I firmly believe that the road to achieving your greatest potential lies in working to heal your inner child. **Some of the benefits of this include:**

- **Improving your happiness and success** through dialogue with your inner child, who can offer valuable insights that help you to perceive right action in a variety of situations.
- **Becoming the person you wish to be.** Your path to wholeness requires that you reconnect with your heart. This is the sacred part of you that holds the key to your spontaneity, your ability to trust, and your ability to give and receive love.

- **Getting to know your inner child allows you to reclaim the power and sanctity of your innermost being,** including your emotions. This allows you to feel more connected with yourself, enabling you to create more meaningful relationships with others as well.

I believe that **your overall level of awareness and degree of emotional competence is grounded in the experiences of your inner child.** The work you do to heal your inner child plucks the resonant chords of your emotional memory, releasing psychic energy that has been trapped in long-forgotten childhood experiences.

I believe that **when you explore and expand your relationship with yourself, you are giving yourself the gift of a whole new mind.** You enhance your success by becoming aware of and changing subconscious emotional programmes, **so you can see the world with new eyes and remember that you were born to win.**

I believe that **you can be no better with others than you are with yourself, so it pays to invest time and energy to improve your relationship with yourself.** I believe that healing your emotional wounds by working with your inner child is key to this process.

Your inner child's mind is full of creativity that transcends the limitations of your conscious awareness. It speaks to you in images that probe your soul, unveil the power within you, shed light on darkness and unleash a new understanding of your desires and dissatisfactions as well as your patterns of behaviour in love, communication, and conflict. When you let go and trust that your conscious and unconscious minds are working together, **your inner child work will not fail to bring out the greatness within you.**

As coaches, Raymond and I have both had the privilege of facilitating many individuals in getting to know their inner child, and watching this process bring out the greatness within. The vast majority of clients I have worked with in this way report that it was one of the most profound moments of transformation in their life. It takes courage and commitment to dig deep, but a skilled facilitator can make it much more effective for you. I am here to support you when you're ready to dive in!

Chapter 2
Emotional Intelligence

*Emotional aptitude is a "meta-ability," determining
how well we can use whatever other skills we have,
including raw intellect.*
*- Daniel Goleman, Emotional Intelligence:
Why It Can Matter More Than IQ*

When author Daniel Goleman literally wrote the book on emotional intelligence, or EQ for short, it sparked a movement among organisational leaders worldwide to pay more attention to this previously under-valued skillset. While many people already had an intuitive understanding of the ideas Dr. Goleman covers in the book, his efforts to track down and lay out the science behind EQ forced even the most recalcitrant managers to pay attention. The book spent a year and half on the bestseller lists and, by the time sales finally slowed, the world of management had been changed forever. Dr. Goleman's subsequent writings on social intelligence and other topics have added even more fuel to the thought revolution already underway.

Raymond and I believe it's no coincidence that this explosion in awareness of emotional intelligence has coincided with an explosion in demand for coaching services. A central insight from Goleman's work is that self-awareness is key to an individual's ability to create better outcomes for themselves and those they manage, and one role of a professional coach is to facilitate clients in expanding their self-awareness. As more leaders have experienced the power of coaching, they have become more committed to self-growth work in general, and to learning tools to increase self-awareness in particular. They have realised the power of EQ to bring out the best in themselves, their colleagues, and those they manage.

Why is Emotional Intelligence Important for Managers?

It takes character and control to be understanding and forgiving.
– Dale Carnegie

Good relationships and coping strategies are invaluable to your success in every area of human activity, from initial bonding with your parents to your ability as a manager to create the space for people to be their best and bring out their creativity and potential. A significant emotional intelligence breakthrough occurred in the 1080s as a result of Dr. Reuven Bar-On's work in the field of emotional intelligence. He was puzzled by some key questions, to illustrate a few:

Why do some people possess greater emotional wellbeing?

Why are some better able to achieve success in life?

Why do some people who are blessed with superior intellectual abilities seem to fail in life, while others with more modest gifts succeed?

Key elements of emotional intelligence consist of:

Self-Awareness, knowing what you are feeling in the moment and using those preferences to guide your decision-making, **Self Management,** managing your emotions so that they help rather than hinder the task at hand, **Social Awareness,** sensing what people are feeling and being able to understand their point of view and, finally **Relationship Management,** guiding, motivating, leading and influencing others.

It is widely understood that that when you are emotionally intelligent you become aware of your emotional experience and you know what you are feeling most of the time. You also have the capacity to recognise how your feelings and emotions impact on your personal opinions, attitudes and judgements. In addition, you will find that, being emotionally intelligent, you may tend to focus on the following competencies:

- Your ability to recognise and understand emotions and express your feelings non-destructively.
- Your ability to understand how others feel and in so doing you relate to others cooperatively.
- Your ability to manage and control emotions effectively.
- Your ability to manage change and the emotions generated by change and to adapt to solving problems

personal and inter-personal.

- Your ability to generate positive effect and be self-motivated.

It is more important for you to be emotionally intelligent because it is consistently agreed across the literature that emotionally intelligent people tend to perform better in various aspects of life than do people who are less emotionally intelligent.

Emotional intelligence has an impact on your career; for example, if you have weaknesses in your Emotional Intelligence, you can seriously harm your career. A study of executives showed that 75% of the reasons why careers become derailed lies in the foundation of weaknesses in Emotional Intelligence.

Among the primary causes of career failure are **poor interpersonal skills, not being a good player and difficulties in handling change.** Nearly all jobs require people to be able to work together effectively in teams. Hence emotionally-intelligent employees are much sought after.

A high intellect alone will rarely propel you to career success in the 21st Century. Many managers are very effective because they are highly emotionally intelligent, despite having average or less than average intellectual ability.

If you have high levels of Emotional Intelligence, good intellectual abilities and good technical skills, you are very well placed for career success. In addition, studies indicate that your Emotional Intelligence is not fixed and tends to increase as you become older, as you are able to draw on a deeper reservoir of life experience.

What differentiates star performance from the rest?

A study cited in Emotional Intelligence and Your Success[1] highlighted that the United States Air Force identified a problem with its recruitment and retention. Approximately 50% of recruiters were leaving employment within a short period of time. The Air Force followed up by participating in a large study that examined the role of emotional intelligence and the impact on recruitment and retention. The research compared self-reported emotional intelligence data and actual performance data with other data. The results showed that many of the same components were correlated. The five factors that were most likely to be translated into success were: assertiveness, empathy, happiness, self-awareness and problem-solving. Focus on the recruitment and retention of new employees involved a follow-up study after one year. The study consisted of the use of emotional intelligence testing in conjunction with specifically developed emotional intelligence interviews with the aim to improve the retention. Worldwide retention improved by 92%, at a cost savings to the Air Force of an estimated $2.7M.[2]

How many organisations are taking notice of a person's ability to cope with stress?

In 1992 the CBI calculated that in the UK, 360 million working days were lost annually through sickness at a cost to organisations of £8 billion.[3] By 2003 the CBI estimate was closer to £11.6 billion and in 2004 reached £12.25 billion. The CBI puts the total cost to the economy of mental health and stress problems at £5 billion a year.[4] *The ability to withstand adverse events and stressful situations without developing physical or emotional symptoms by actively coping with stress is a necessary requirement for leaders and employees.* This ability is based on three competencies:

1. The capacity to choose courses of action for dealing with stress (being resourceful and effective, being able to come up with suitable methods, knowing what to do and how to do it).

2. An optimistic disposition toward new experiences and change in general, and one's ability to successfully overcome the specific problem at hand.

3. A feeling that one can control or influence the stressful situation by staying calm and maintaining control.[5]

Dr. Martyn Newman explains that in creating optimism one needs to look on the brighter side of life as well as sense opportunities. Even in the face of adversity is imperative to have a sense of positivity and well-being. Treating yourself kindly, or simply trusting that you can eventually achieve your goals, are all optimism strategies. Other ways to become more optimistic include:

- When faced with a challenging situation, look for the positive benefit. Step back from the perceived crisis and recast it not as a catastrophe and a threat but as a challenge and an opportunity.

- Seek the valuable lesson in every problem or difficulty.

- Let go of the negative emotion that events cause and, instead, focus on the task to be accomplished.[6]

I find **The Optimist Creed** – By Christian D Larson to be most inspiring:

I Promise Myself......
To be so strong that nothing can disturb my peace of mind.
To take health, happiness, and prosperity to every person I meet.
To make all my friends feel that there is something in them.
To look at the sunny side of everything and make my optimism come true.
To think only of the best, to work only for the best, and to expect only the best.
To be just as enthusiastic about the success of others as I am about my own.
To forget the mistakes of the past and press on to the greater achievements of the future.
To wear a cheerful countenance at all times and give every living creature I meet a smile.
To give so much time to the improvement of myself that I have no time to criticize others.
To be too large for worry, too noble for anger, too strong for fear, and too happy to permit the presence of trouble.

To think well of myself and proclaim this fact to the world, not in loud words but in great deeds.
To live in the faith that the whole world is on my side so long as I am true to the best that is in me.

Kate Cannon's work at American Express Financial Services[7], stating that emotional skills can be improved in the work environment, is well documented. Kate designed a programme to improve Emotional Intelligence. The outcome of the programme was that sales staff showed improvement in their performance at work, and that many of the same staff reported greater success in dealing with situations that arose in their personal lives. Within the aforementioned study group the Emotional Intelligence factors that showed the most change, especially among those who initially scored low, were assertiveness, empathy, reality testing, self-actualisation, self-regard and optimism.

It is widely understood in management circles today that trust is the glue that holds relationships together. Creating and maintaining trust is the foundation of effective management, and it requires a certain level of emotional intelligence on the part of both leaders and team members. Often, our hidden concern centres on not knowing what will be expected of us by others. Trust is built when agendas are revealed and expectations shared. When trust is lacking within a relationship, there will be behaviours motivated by caution and façade. When issues relating to trust are openly addressed, however, the relationship is strengthened by mutual regard and forthrightness. The spontaneous flow and exchange of information among the people within the relationship signifies that this is a trusting relationship.

The building of trust must include the following three features for it to be effective:

Mutual Regard

When people share mutual regard, they view one another as reliable, competent and trustworthy. The environment within which the relationship occurs is positive, and persons are non-manipulative and mutually supportive. They take what one another says at face value, so there is little questioning of the motives or intentions of the other.

Forthrightness

A primary expression of trust is the willingness to be open and transparent in our dealings with other persons. Forthrightness involves disclosing all relevant information, as well as full authenticity in being that encourages people to say what they think, feel and see. Persons are direct and up-front with one another, feeling little reason to hold back. Dr. Martyn Newman states that emotionally-intelligent leaders express their feelings and points of view in a straightforward way, while respecting the fact that others may hold a different opinion or expectation. Such leaders are comfortable challenging the views of others, and are therefore unafraid to give clear messages.

Spontaneous Interaction

Persons who operate at high levels of trust are able to be spontaneous, rather than calculated or measured in their interactions. Personal feedback is given directly, and others within the relationship are able to address the underlying issues. Persons are not overly concerned about making a mistake or offending someone else, hence there is free and clear communication.

I believe that it is extremely important to spend time building trust, in order to enhance and have extraordinary outcomes in relationships. Signs of unresolved trust show up as:

Caution

Where there is little trust, people tend to think hard before speaking, play it close to the chest, and do not take any chances within the relationship. In situations where there is lack of trust, a person hesitates to put her or himself in a position where s/he feels vulnerable to the other person.

Mistrust

When there is mistrust of one person in relation to the other, the other person is not viewed as reliable or trustworthy. A person may assume that that the other does not have her/his best interests at heart, and may be more likely to put self-interest above the collective whole. In such situations, the person who holds mistrust is guarded and attentive to any perceived aggression from the other.

In addition, there may be suspicion of the motives of others and sensitivity to hidden agendas.

This is one reason why more companies have begun to include assessments of emotional intelligence in employment screening procedures. As the quote from Dale Carnegie suggests, for managers, creating trust involves striking an ideal balance between empathy and firm standards. Team members need to know that you will not react emotionally to any bad news they may present you with, but will listen with cool-headed focus and make your assessments and decisions from that place of empathy and emotional control. When those who work for you know they can count on you to be fair, authentic and transparent, they will trust you enough to stay in communication when problems arise.

While emotional intelligence is vital to the creation of productive relationships with the people you manage, it is equally important in your relationships with your peers. Ineffective or adversarial relationships between leaders negatively affect the performance of each individual involved and the organisation as a whole. Lack of harmony and effective communication at the top also impacts morale, and can damage the reputation and bottom line of the organisation. This is why John D. Rockefeller said:

The ability to deal with people is as purchasable a commodity as sugar or coffee, and I will pay more for that ability than for any other thing under the sun.

His prescient understanding of the fundamental importance of emotional intelligence for organisational performance is no doubt largely responsible for his status as one of history's most successful businessmen. He intuitively knew that these skills were well worth paying a premium for when hiring people to whom he entrusted the management of his complex and highly-profitable business. I find the following quote from him equally enlightening:

Good leadership consists of showing average people how to do the work of superior people.

It is as if he is saying indirectly that maximizing individual performance is a matter of revealing the greatness within each team member, so they can see their own potential and produce exceptional work as a result. This is a core premise of the transformational leadership movement that has taken the world by storm in recent years, and he had already discovered it nearly a century ago.

The most successful leaders have always known that creating effective relationships with people whose input and collaboration you need to achieve your desired outcomes makes good corporate sense. Poor relationship between leaders and those being led can damage the performance of teams, lower individual members' self-esteem, damage reputation as well as the financial bottom line of an organisation, because poor relationships affect performance and strategic outcomes.

Here are just a few of the ways that cultivating emotional intelligence and good relationship skills can help you lead more effectively. EQ allows you to:

- Manage conflict skilfully.
- Build more productive relationships with people at all levels, from fellow managers to custodial staff.
- Develop intra- and inter-personal intelligence to navigate your relationships with yourself and others more smoothly.
- Focus on creating ideal team relationships and improving measurable outcomes.
- Be effective with diverse individuals, groups and cultures.
- Increase your understanding and acceptance of both yourself and others.
- Be effective in your personal relationships, preserving that which you value within the relationship.

Dr. Martyn Newman the author of Emotional Capitalist – The New Leaders says that: *today's global interactions require people in organisations to form relationships, share goals and work collaboratively to achieve those goals.* In response to this, the concept of a team as a static entity is giving way to a new understanding of teams as networks of interdependent relationships. When you dedicate time and energy to developing your emotional intelligence skills as a manager, you increase your ability to safely and efficiently navigate the turbulent waters of modern working relationships to successfully reach the shore of your strategic outcomes.

Building Relationships

Building relationships is a skill that is about consciously managing and developing the most valuable asset a company or person possesses. Relationships represent a unique strategic resource.
– Dr. Martyn Newman, <u>Emotional Capitalists: The New Leaders</u>

Building relationship capital requires understanding and identifying the key relationships in your business, then using practical strategies for leveraging them to improve outcomes. Good relationships with a wide range of people are usually necessary, and there are specific skills that can be learned to improve social effectiveness.

The first such skill involves becoming aware of the work and social environment, so you can learn to discern when, where and why to begin and end each interaction.

The second set of skills involves polishing interpersonal skills, and covers both verbal and non-verbal aspects of personal interactions such as how to be a good listener, how to change topics, and how to keep a conversation focussed.

The third set of skills involved in building effective work relationships centres on presentation skills.

Dr. Martyn Newman, author of the book <u>Emotional Capitalists</u>, draws attention to the following: No business, regardless of its size or industry, can function without collaborative relationships because they provide the context in which people do business. As a manager or CEO, your task is to engage the hearts and minds of your people so that they are inspired to deliver superior service and perform at their best.

Building Relationship Capital

Trust is the glue of life. It's the most essential ingredient in effective communication. It's the foundational principle that holds all relationships. – Stephen R. Covey

It is one thing to work on our own emotional intelligence skills as leaders, but it's quite another to facilitate those we manage in doing the same. Your team members will not feel safe to change in such fundamental, intimate ways unless you work hard to establish trust between them, as well as in you.

To do this, you need concrete tools with which to ground the concepts of emotional intelligence into practical reality. Such tools can be found in a variety of sources, but one of the people who has done the most to promote the practical application of EQ principles in organisations is Dr. Martyn Newman, whose background as a psychological researcher has given him the clout to assert the value of building emotional capital to CEOs worldwide.

In an article entitled *7 Tips for Building Your Emotional Wealth*, Dr. Newman summarizes what he's learned in over 15 years spent putting his knowledge of emotional intelligence to work for organizations:

The evidence is impressive. The research ... has established clear links between happiness and our health, wealth and wellbeing. By happiness I mean an emotional, physical and spiritual prosperity – something I call Emotional Capital.

In light of these insights, it's clear that a business relationship must fulfil the following three conditions to be effective:

Equality

Relationships work best when people are recognised and treated as equals. As a manager, you need to find common ground because, ultimately, everything depends on the quality of your relationships with the people you manage. When those you lead feel recognised and valued by you, they will be inspired to do their best work. Make sure they know you're available for them and that your role is to remove any barriers that prevent them from maximizing their productivity.

Mutuality

People collaborate with you and work well for you when you provide benefits for them in return. When you look for ways to get what you want by giving the people who work for you something they want as well, everyone wins. A little give-and-take goes a long way towards keeping your team members motivated, and people naturally want to give back to those who give to them.

Empowerment

When you give people the space to make their maximum contribution to your work together, they will go the extra mile and take pride in the results. When you let go of micro-managing, you give people freedom and a sense of ownership in the relationship. In the same way that young children get immense satisfaction out of being allowed to complete tasks without adult interference, everyone feels happier with their work when they are allowed the greatest possible amount of autonomy.

***

Over and over again in our careers as executive coaches, with me logging over 25 years on corporate boards, including 10 years as chairman, Raymond and I have seen the results that come when leaders prioritize building relationship capital. When you take the time to hone emotional intelligence in yourself and those you manage, you are creating fertile soil in which enhanced productivity and outcomes can grow.

[1] Emotional Intelligence and Your Success, Steven J. Stein and Howard E. Book. Josey Bass 2006, Chapter 18 p.

[2] United States General Accounting Office, Testimony before the Subcommittee on Military Personnel, committee on National Security, House of Representatives, Military Attrition: DOD Needs to Better Analyse Reasons for Separation and Improving Recruiting Systems, March 12, 1998, (GAO/T-NSIAD-98-117)

[3] **"Stress Prevention in the Workplace - Assessing the Costs and Benefits to Organisation"** by Prof. Cary L. Cooper and Dr. Susan Cartwright (both of Manchester School of Management, UMIST); Prof. Paula Liukkonen, Department of Economics, University of Stockholm, Sweden.
Published by the European Foundation for the Improvement of Living and Working Conditions

[4] ibid

[5] Definition adapted from R. Bar-On. *BarOn Emotional Quotient Inventory Technical Manual* (Toronto: Multi-Health Systems 1997), p. 18-19

[6] Martyn Newman, Emotional Capitalist: The New Leaders – Building Emotional Intelligence and Leadership Success. Jossey-Bass, 2007

[7] Kate Cannon, Personal Communication, 1998: G. Sitarenios Pre-Analysis: American Express Co. Employees (Toronto: Multi-Health Systems, 1998. See also Tony Schwartz, "How Do You Feel?" Fast Company, 35 (June 2000) p. 296

Chapter 3
Clarity Produces Results

When you are clear, what you want will show up in your life, and only to the extent you are clear. – Janet Bray Attwood

I know that the value of my service as a coach comes in large part from my ability to help people reach clarity regarding both their goals and the obstacles they face in achieving them. I have seen countless examples in my work of how a lack of clarity in any of these areas can cause stagnation and a drop in performance in every area of life. It is as if a dam has been erected in the river of the client's life, stopping the flow of their life force and leaving them feeling stuck and hopeless.

Often, people who have been struggling in this way for some time when they come to me have begun to blame themselves, unable to uncover the source of their dissatisfaction. In such cases, I always remind them that everyone goes through such periods of confusion at one time or another, and that very few are able to get through them without support.

This is simply because human nature makes it very difficult for us to see our own blocks; it's like trying to see your own face without a mirror. By hiring a coach, they have shown that they are serious about their own fulfilment and ready to commit to growth in service to their highest aspirations for their lives. It is my privilege to have witnessed many people living into this as a result of my work to establish clarity. This happens regularly because, as Janet Attwood's quote suggests, clarity is the key to activating the Law of Attraction in your life.

This is why I wish to address clarity in this book about relationships: because the Law of Attraction tells us that our thoughts create our reality, including all of our interactions with others. Clarity produces results because it is your mental attitude towards life that determines the quality of your experiences with the people you encounter. In my own transpersonal development I have been coached to expect nothing, and experience everything. That way I am opened to a multitude of possibilities underpinned by the clarity of focusing on how I am being, and the possibility that I am creating for myself and my life.

When you are clear about what you want, however, you allow it to come to you in unexpected and glorious ways. The universe will appear random and unresponsive only to the extent that you believe it is, and to the extent that you fail to be clear.

This is why, if you wish to reach your maximum potential, you must continually work to heal your inner child, build your emotional capital, and otherwise optimize your relationships with yourself and others. How you feel, think and act is an indication of who you are being, and this is what the Law of Attraction responds to.

Simon Hedley, Strategist Alchemist, says *I have learnt that clarity is an access to real power and as we teach and apply The Merlin Method (that is, starting with the end in mind), having clarity to such a level that you have an understanding of how everything could be and optimally can be. Having clarity on what you are prepared to commit to and to produce to make all the difference. My banking and audit experience has taught me how a single penny can and does make the difference over time and how so many people make huge assumptions setting themselves and others up for failure.*

Simon is cognizant of the success spiral and he has noticed and commented that *some people flow as they journey towards success in diverse areas of life; from harnessing their finances, their relationships, opportunities and connections. He has observed that things seem to come easily to people with mind-sets that cultivate flow. Rather than moving in a linear straight line, some people move through their lives with ease and luck, like dolphins surfacing in the flow.*

Simon and his partners have spent decades becoming connected to, spending time with, modeling, and discussing these ideas with exceptional people who produce success. People whose results he personally finds miraculous range from philanthropic billionaires, to award-winning musicians, to sports superstars to entrepreneurs who produce global change. He notes that the key factor that underpins success for them all is clarity, and this unshakable clarity informs The Success Spiral™.

In an interview with Simon, he articulates that you can't work with and master something you don't know about, and that upon reflection, he realized how much he had missed in the days before he was aware of The Success Spiral™. With exuberance, he explains *what excites me is what is now possible for us all now once we use what we learn from inquiring into The Success Spiral™.*

Know what you want, so you can receive it

You cannot solve a problem from the same consciousness that created it. You must learn to see the world anew.
-- *Albert Einstein*

When you are faced with a problem of any kind, the first step to solving it must be to establish clarity about what you do want, so you can put your attention there. I believe that this is what Einstein meant by learning to 'see the world anew,' because getting to clarity requires letting go of your focus on what is wrong. The Law of Attraction tells us that we always get more of what we focus our attention on; thus we cannot receive the solution while our attention remains focused on the problem. The trick is to expand your awareness to a much wider scope, so you can hold the problem within a field that also allows the solution to emerge.

Of all the people I have learnt of and encountered in my years spent facilitating transformation, there is one person who stands out in her embodiment of this idea. Her name is Alice Herz Sommer, and she is the subject of a book called *A Garden of Eden in Hell*. In it she relates how she managed to not only survive over two years in a Nazi concentration camp, but go on to thrive well into her 11th decade. She finally passed away in February 2014 at age 110, having lived independently and played her beloved piano daily up until the end.

In addition to the book, she offered profound wisdom from her long life in numerous interviews, including one with Anthony Robbins, as well as a short documentary film called *The Lady in Number 6* which won an Oscar in 2013.

In the interview with Tony Robbins, he asks her how she managed to stay optimistic even as she was surrounded by squalor, suffering and death at Terezin concentration camp. Her answer was:

I look at the good. When you are relaxed, your body is always relaxed. When you are pessimistic, your body behaves in an unnatural way. It is up to us whether we look at the good or the bad. When you are nice to others, they are nice to you. When you give, you receive...Everything is a present.

She goes on to explain how, since childhood, she has intuitively known that optimism was the key to a happy life. Her story becomes even more intriguing when she relates that she was born a twin, and her twin sister was the opposite of her from the beginning, constantly complaining and focusing on what was wrong. Alice's sister predeceased her by many decades, and this does not surprise Alice in the least.

Neither should we be surprised that decades of research by Dr. Martyn Newman and others have shown that optimism is one of the ten most important competencies in the development of emotional intelligence.

I find the following statement profound in regard to the power of an optimistic and clear mind:

One of the first things we learn when we pay attention to the quiet voice of the subconscious mind is that as soon as the problem arises, the solution is born. The problem appears before the conscious mind while the solution hides in the subconscious mind. Through the subconscious mind we can know the solution as soon as we encounter the problem. Without such insight we spend our energies pursuing the problem and finally becoming identified with it. Although we may declare that we are looking for a solution, we are actually hanging onto the problem and not allowing it to transform itself into its alter ego, the solution.
Jack Schwarz, The Path of Action

Successful people are problem solvers, but to achieve your goals you must hone your ability to change your perspective when faced with a problem. It helps to recognize that there is no problem you could ever encounter that the universe cannot provide a solution for, if you are open to it.

Successful people make it their business to hold in their minds the images and ideals of the results they wish to realise, and they trust that this will activate the power of the Universe to make their dreams a reality. Such people never doubt that keeping their focus on their vision will eventually allow a solution to be revealed.

Create Inner Clarity to Achieve Outer Harmony

Life desires expression through you, and it is your business to express yourself with clarity in a harmonious and constructive way. When you embody integrity and truth in your relationship with yourself, your external reality will adjust to match the poise and harmony within. I have often enjoyed witnessing this transformation in my coaching clients. A powerful clarity lies within you just waiting to be revealed, and my job is simply to facilitate you in uncovering it. My clients often tell me that there is no greater feeling than the realization that the answers have been within themselves all along.

When we understand and accept the Law of Attraction, we know with certainty that happy relationships cannot exist with an unhappy consciousness.

Therefore, if you want pleasant and productive relationships, you must do what you can to change your 'point of attraction' by changing your thoughts. Since beliefs are only thoughts that you repeatedly think, it follows that consciously changing your beliefs will positively impact your point of attraction.

At Beacon Organisational Development, we lead clients through a powerful 6-step One Command™ process developed by Asara Lovejoy, to help them access and change the subconscious beliefs that are largely responsible for any lack of clarity or success they may experience. It is vital to make these changes, because as Charles Haanel points out in his book The Master Key System:

Thought is a spiritual activity and therefore creative, [but] thought will create nothing unless it is consciously, systematically and constructively directed.

Nowadays, there are innumerable coaches and consultants offering services to help clients effect transformation at the personal and organisational level. However, not all the tools they use for this purpose are equally effective, and this is why you want to work with coaches like Raymond or myself who have a proven track record in facilitating deep transformation.

With the right tools and the proper support, it is amazing how quickly you can replace disempowering beliefs with thoughts that return you to a state of clarity and flow. It is as if the old, unconscious beliefs literally take up space in your energy field, and must be cleaned out to make space for new, consciously chosen ones.

Robert Collier says, *It is the belief that you have in yourself that counts. It is the consciousness of dominant power within you that makes all things attainable. You can do anything you think you can. This knowledge is literally the gift of the Gods, for through it you can solve every human problem. It should make you an incurable optimist. It is the open door to welfare. Keep it open by expecting to gain everything that is right. You are entitled to everything that is good. Therefore, expect nothing but good. Defeat does not have to follow victory. You don't have to "knock wood" every time you congratulate yourself that things have been going well with you.*

I have learnt and seen exceptional miracles in my life where victory follows victory, and it will for you too if you let your mind-set flow with love, peace, harmony, compassion and effortless ease. In my own transpersonal growth, each time I get in the grip of emotional baggage, my coach gives me one word only – BREATHE. This too, shall pass, and the breath will take us through.

With unshakable clarity, bring all your thoughts, your desires, your aims, your talents into the consciousness of the storehouse of good which is the law of infinite supply, and give gratitude for the blessings. There is every reason to know that you are entitled to adequate provision. Everything that is involved in supply is a product of thought. So reach out, stretch your mind, and try to comprehend unlimited thought and unlimited supply.

Clarity is about Vibration

I have already spoken a bit about the role of the Law of Attraction in the creation of harmonious relationships, so I'd like to take that line of thinking a step further and suggest that *clarity is all about vibration*. In this context, *vibration* refers to a quality of being that we can't easily define, but which seems to be correlated with our emotions. Tools such as meditation, visualisation, and affirmation allow you to change your vibration to consciously create your reality. It is also important to remember that love is the greatest power on earth and it has the highest vibration.

When you approach each relationship with love for what is within the relationship, loving how the relationship is and how it is not, a clear vibration is released, the stage is set for synchronicities and other little miracles to happen almost effortlessly.

When you take the time to become clear prior to a meeting, it's as if the others involved unconsciously attune themselves to your clarity, and leave their own confusions and doubts at the door. The meeting is productive because each person stays focussed and on-task throughout, and there is a flow to your communications that makes maximum use of the allotted time. As a leader, you have the privilege and responsibility of 'setting the space' for the entire group, and when you take that responsibility seriously, everyone benefits.

People will start to leave your meetings feeling energised instead of drained, and will be puzzled because they can't put their finger on what changed. This becomes great fun to watch as you gain practice with it!

Gain all the clarity in the world that the relationship you have with yourself and the Universal Mind is of utmost importance. The Universal Mind expresses itself through you, and it is continually seeking an outlet.

The Universal Mind is like a vast reservoir of water, constantly replenished by the rain. Open your channel (that is, your thoughts and where you focus them) to the Universal Mind, and its water will flow in ever-increasing volume. In parallel, once you open a channel of service that serves humankind in the highest and best way, the Universal Mind has no other direction than to express itself through you. Then the gifts of the Universal Mind will flow in ever-increasing volume and you will be enriched in the process, just like a banker providing the necessary resources to make your life productive.

Chapter 4
Negotiation as a Creative Process

Creative negotiating is a process whereby two or more partners meet and, through artful discussion and creativity, confront a problem and arrive at an innovative solution that best meets the needs of all parties and secures their commitment to fulfilling the agreement reached.
– Gordon Shea, Creative Negotiating

Good business leaders know that skilful negotiation is central to their ability to consistently produce the results they want for themselves and their companies. Many understand that, as with most things, this skillset gets easier with practice, so they work to fine-tune their negotiation skills in service of their objectives. Still, even the most accomplished leaders may still feel a certain amount of trepidation when the subject of negotiation arises. This may be because they associate negotiation with conflict, and how many people can truly say that they welcome conflict?

Yet, as the quote from Gordon Shea makes clear, this is a limited perception of a subject that becomes much more attractive when it is viewed instead as a creative process.

Many people who are living in advanced, modern economies are sometimes confused as to what exactly they want.

To a large extent the sheer abundance of options offered in the marketplace presents difficulties to people in terms of choice. Dr Habib Chamount-Nicholás, in his book Negotiate like a Phoenician, illustrates that the Phoenicians focused not so much on price, but on more intangible benefits, which are more valuable than generally believed. The Phoenicians focused on creating friendships with their business partners, referring to the friendship between Solomon and Hiram as an example.

The lesson for you today as a business person, entrepreneur or leader within an organisation is that you will benefit from working in creative ways to solve your client's needs, because often those needs are external to the negotiation being conducted. The way to discover your customer's unstated needs is simply to ask, and then listen. The quality of the interaction, and therefore of the results, is determined by the listening.

In coming to a negotiated deal it is important to have clarity on what is negotiable, what is not negotiable, and what does not need to be negotiated. That is why planning the negotiation is so important. The planning involves the following steps:

Step 1. Identifying your wants. This is what I want, this is what the other party can offer. This is what the other party wants, this is what I can offer. Then clarifying and noting the key wants for both yourself and the other party. Having had a clear sense of what the other party might want, then move on to...

Step 2. Set objectives. It is important to hold the objectives and possibilities for the negotiation in mind.

Step 3. Your next step is to have a fall-back position, the best alternative for win/win outcomes. Your fall-back position will govern your perception of your own power in the negotiation. It also governs the other party's perception of your power.

Step 4. Identify your tradeables – which issues can you bargain with? Follow this with an assessment of how valuable your tradeables are to you and to the other party. Trading your limits – Set your best and worse limits. Your best limit is the agreement for your tradeable which will still give the other party the perception that they have achieved a reasonable agreement under the circumstances, and the litmus step is, will the other party be inclined to do future business with you?

Step 5. Always be prepared for diverse experiences. Regardless of how much planning you do, the nature of being human means that you need to anticipate everything from the other party. So ask yourself several "What if" questions and plan creative options that may be used to keep negotiation away from deadlock and complete breakdown. It is wise to include in your research probabilities such as the arithmetic approach and the creative approach, as outlined below.

The arithmetic approach is the principle of bargaining to trade concessions, but this only works if the other party perceives your concessions as having roughly equal value to theirs. To identify areas where you can trade in this way is to look for issues which are low priority to you and high priority to the other party. The other party will do the same, hence it is the whole principle of trading concessions.

The creative approach goes beyond the arithmetic approach in the sense that it looks for proposals that you may make, which give you net gain when traded for a concession from the other party; to that end they need to be low value to you and high value to the other party. Creative approaches require you to ask questions, think laterally and search for possibilities to create win/win outcomes.

Step 6. The final step is to conclude. As soon as you arrive at the best win/win deal that is available, you want to wrap up the proceedings and get on with the implementation. Until there is commitment to the written agreement, things can go wrong, so you want to ensure that:

- The terms of the final agreement are understood by both parties.
- The terms will not be changed before they are converted into a formal contract and implemented.

In order to achieve the terms of the final agreement you need to:

- Summarise – One party or the other must summarise the terms of the agreement on all the tradeables and gain the other party's commitment that the summary is accurate and complete.
- Write it down – the key terms of the agreement must be committed to paper. Handwritten notes will do, provided both parties leave with a copy of the same documents.

Perhaps we conflate negotiation with conflict in part because our daily experience of it is fairly limited in the industrialised world. When we do find ourselves in a high-stakes negotiation, it can activate internal defence mechanisms that may actually work against us. However, low-stakes negotiation is a routine part of life in developing economies worldwide, where the procurement of goods and services often involves bartering. In open-air plazas and arcades in countries across Africa, Asia, and South America, those who sell goods and those who purchase them enjoy the stimulating challenge of negotiating amongst themselves, sometimes for hours, until they arrive at a price that is satisfactory to each. While the details of the bartering ritual vary from country to country, participants will often appear to be arguing in earnest as they attempt to 'win the game.' For these 'contestants,' there is usually a certain amount of entertainment value in the process, as well as relationship building. Because bartering is an integral part of the socioeconomic fabric of such cultures, both parties usually feel that resources expended in negotiation are well spent.

Of course, in today's modern business world time is money, and you may not have the luxury of spending hours to negotiate every issue, nor would you want to. However, we can still take a page from the book of the world's bazaar denizens and bring a lighter approach to the negotiating table. Conflict and compromise may be inevitable, but that doesn't mean that the process of negotiation must be unpleasant.

You are most likely already familiar with the following five strategies for engaging in negotiations, but they are worth reviewing:

1. Win-Win
Espoused as the ideal approach by many management consultants today, this model is characterised by respect for the differences in each negotiating party's values. In win-win situations, decision-making is synergistic, meaning that each additional value system that comes into play actually increases the potential for high-quality results, rather than obstructing progress. The focus is not on who is right, but what is right. This has roots in the same utilitarian ethical philosophy that underlies democratic legislative processes.

2. Win-Lose
In this model, both parties are motivated chiefly by competitive self-interest, with one party eventually prevailing over another. In this situation, decision-making is primarily influenced by the victorious party, because, as Churchill observed, 'history is written by the victors.' We often see this in nature when, after a prolonged chase, the

exhausted prey gives up hope and allows the predator to move in for the kill.

3. Lose-Win

This model is characterised by no evidence of collaboration or competition, but rather by the surrender of one party to another. Again, decision-making is primarily influenced by one party. The surrendering party may feel deflated and disempowered at the least, or in extreme cases oppressed.

4. Lose-Lose

In this scenario, the relationship between parties is characterised by interpersonal conflict to such an extent that those involved are constantly defending their values in an adversarial manner, whilst the common purpose is side-lined. Both parties waste time and other resources due to a mutual unwillingness to respect each other's values.

5. No-Way

This scenario is characterized by agreement amongst all parties involved that there is no way that certain key issues can be mutually agreed upon. While the relationship may continue in one of the four other paradigms to resolve unrelated issues, it eventually becomes clear that there is no possibility of compromise on one or more areas of disagreement. When this fundamental problem is acknowledged, a decision to terminate the relationship is made for the mutual benefit of all involved, with the issue in question being 'tabled' so the parties can concentrate on the win-win aspects of the relationship. This scenario is frequently seen in the legislative process of countries like the United States, where the political sphere is dominated by two parties that are sharply divided ideologically.

These are all familiar negotiation scenarios that have been around since the dawn of humanity. However, the field of *creative negotiation* gives us new ways to 'expand the pie' so that the parties involved can each receive at least *some* portion of what they want, and thus feel that a genuine effort has been made to meet their needs. This is particularly crucial to maintain goodwill when the need to negotiate with the parties is ongoing. Like so much of business, creative negotiation is absolutely dependent on clear communication and sound relationship skills. There must be a commitment to empathy and mutual respect among all parties involved, and this will be greatly enhanced when attention has been given to the relationship over time. Of course this is not always possible; there are times when we must negotiate high-stakes deals with people we have never met before and will never see again, who may even come from cultures very different from our own. However, this is more the exception than the rule for most of us, and even in such situations a high degree of emotional intelligence will augment your effectiveness as a negotiator.

As we manage our relationships and increase our emotional intelligence, we learn how we differ from others, and we identify our unique strengths. At the same time, we also identify our blind spots and accept our limitations, knowing that we are always a part of something larger. At the most basic level, the negotiations we engage in with all our relationships teach us to create, and this includes our relationship with ourselves. When we commit to bringing caring and authenticity to all our interactions with one another, we are creating bonds whose value is immeasurable.

Your success in any negotiation will be determined by your ability to combine adequate preparation – knowing your objectives, strengths, and what represents a deal-breaker to you – with creativity and emotional intelligence.

When you are clear on the goals that you bring to the negotiating table, you will find it easier to banish your fears of what you might lose so you can stay focused on what it is you hope to gain.

To reflect on poker analogy for a moment, what sets the pros apart is their ability to keep a laser-like focus on their target pay-out despite the risk involved, thereby maintaining what's called *promotion-focus.* This has been shown to be key to success in all types of negotiations: you must keep your attention on what you hope to gain, rather than what you're afraid of losing (*prevention-focus*).

I believe that the best outcome for all parties is achieved when participants are able to *combine* awareness of the issues at hand with awareness of their goals. The difference comes from shifting one's focus from fear of loss, to positive expectation that a creative solution will be found that works for all. Once again, it's the Law of Attraction at work in our everyday lives.

In the kinds of complex, multi-issue negotiations that are commonly encountered in the business world today, it is often possible to 'expand the pie' by taking advantage of differing priorities amongst the parties involved.

If each party is willing to yield on issues that are lower on their list of priorities, then each can potentially find greater satisfaction in the final agreement. This is a keystone in the creative negotiation process.

When you prepare yourself by writing out in detail what you hope to gain in a given negotiation, you will find it easier to stay focused on those objectives as you come to an agreement with other parties involved. When you enter the room believing strongly that a solution exists that works for everyone, you create the space for that solution to be revealed.

Chapter 5
Relationship Intelligence for Conflict Management

Managers need to know how to create teams that feel psychologically safe enough for conflicting opinions to be aired and the benefits of diversity exploited. – Mark de Rond

In my decades of consulting with organisations, I have learnt some valuable lessons regarding conflict, many of which seemed counter-intuitive at the time. In recent years, however, I have seen a refreshing new understanding of conflict begin to blossom within management circles, one that recognises conflict as a normal, even valuable, feature of human interaction.

Indeed, the more intelligent and creative the individuals that make up a team, the more conflict there is likely to be, and the energy that such a dynamic generates can be channelled to great effect by a competent leader.

This kind of thinking is behind the growing chorus of voices advocating the view that too little conflict can be just as bad for business as too much conflict. The question is, how do we foster constructive conflict that supports productivity, rather than destructive conflict that degrades it? The answer has a great deal to do with the structures and expectations put in place by leadership with respect to managing conflict, and these must be informed by emotional intelligence.

The Two Faces of Conflict

Conflict can be divisive, disruptive, and a draining distraction. It is a stress-maker and it can magnify a problem so much that it casts a heavy shadow over the workplace. It is pervasive and insidious, and cannot be contained by the walls of an office – somehow, no matter how tiny the department in which conflict arises, it will infect the rest of the company.

Yet there are many positive aspects of conflict. It precipitates change, and its resolution triggers growth and progress. When conflict finds its rightful place within the life of a group, it releases enormous amounts of energy; it changes the group dynamics and it reveals hidden potential.

The emergence of conflict within your team does not mean you have failed as a leader. Rather, view it as a vote of confidence among your group members that they trust both you and each other enough to be open with such difficult feelings.

Here are some key points for group leaders to remember in the face of conflict:

- Conflict is intrinsic to normal human development, and is a part and parcel of group formation
- Keep calm, and have confidence in your ability to be the crucible in which the feelings of the group are contained
- Don't be afraid to address the conflict as you perceive it
- Have confidence in your feelings, and know that there is no need to apologise for them
- Make sure you have adequate support and have the freedom to explore issues of conflict outside of the group
- Conflict is a catalyst for transformation and for the release of stored energy and potential

Just about everyone approaches conflict differently. Some run away from it, others face it head on while yet others may pretend it doesn't exist. In my experience, there are five different conflict-handling styles. Which is yours?

Avoidance	***Ignoring conflicts in the hope that they will disappear***

  - Putting problems under consideration on hold
  - Invoking slow procedures to stifle the conflict
  - Using secrecy to avoid confrontation
  - Leveraging bureaucratic rules to minimise or camouflage the conflict

Compromise   *Negotiation*
- Looking for deals and trade offs
- Finding satisfactory or acceptable solutions

Competition   *Creating win-lose solutions*
- Using rivalry to play one party against another
- Employing power plays to achieve one's own ends
- Forcing submission

Accommodation   *Giving way*
- Submission and compliance to the stronger party

Collaboration   *Problem solving stance*
- Confronting difference and sharing ideas and information
- Searching for integrative solutions

Collaboration Over Conflict

It is now generally accepted that a collaborative approach to conflict is preferable where circumstances allow, especially when the effects of the decisions made will significantly impact a diverse number of people. Collaborative decision-making can be time-consuming, and requires more attention and energy than top-down strategies for conflict resolution.

However, I believe that investment in a culture of equality, mutuality and empowerment is well worth the time required. With the right tools, structures, and above all with clear communication, you can help your team members begin to understand conflict as the valuable source of growth and progress that it is.

To begin this process, we must return to the subject of the limbic brain. As I touched on earlier, emotional intelligence can only take root and grow in an atmosphere of safety and trust, where the inner child feels seen, heard, and cared for. As a leader, you must understand that most people do not have successful conflict resolution modelled for them as children; indeed, for too many, conflict of any kind is strongly associated with trauma. As a result, many people go immediately into subconscious patterns of self-protection when confronted with even the slightest intimation of conflict.

These are the patterns they formed to protect themselves as small children when their parents fought, or their siblings antagonized them, or the school bully beat them up. As I have discussed, the power of these subconscious patterns is formidable, and healing them requires courage and a willingness to listen to the inner child.

It is my observation in the role of chairman of boards that there are times when others feel cut off from feeling valued. In such situations, a person who feels cut off from achieving their self-worth will deploy purposeful behaviour to defend their self-worth.

The purpose of this conflict style is to regain feelings of self-worth. In such cases, the conflict is a vehicle that is intended to remove resistance to getting to where you want to be. For example, a person who is principled, fair, analytical and cautious – whose reports may be perceived as excessively detailed – may respond in a forceful, competitive manner so she wins the right to continue producing her detailed reports in the future.

When relationships are harmonious she may deploy her behaviour with flexibility, but she may deploy her behaviour in a sequence of styles. The first stage is to brush off the perceived opposition. In the second stage, the purpose is to defend her personal right to hold her view of the issue in question. In the final stage, the purpose may be to capitulate to escape, or to mount the final defence. Each successive style brings an increased urgency to the task of retaining self-worth, and she may feel stressed in the final stage of conflict.

The literature from Personal Strengths Publishing (UK) Ltd sets the position that that there are two kinds of conflict, warranted and unwarranted:

(1) Warranted or real conflict is generated in environments where the person is cut off from access to a relating style that he or she values. This kind of conflict may occur for you when you encounter a situation that makes it impossible for you to achieve the purpose of what you most value in relating to others. The longer the feeling of being cut-off persists despite efforts of being valued, the greater the potential to feel stress.

(2) Unwarranted conflict. This occurs when the shared goal is not in dispute, but the method to reach it is. Here there is no understanding of the preferences of the other person. Imagine a Board of Directors who want to agree on a process of implementing a redundancy programme, when each has a different personal value-based system.

Unwarranted conflict can quickly become the scenario in which: each learns of the perspectives of others; each improves personal objectivity; each is able to contribute in a challenging way but awareness of the need to respect the value of others; resolution emerging in which the result of cumulative enhancing of each others' perspectives. In such situations decisions are made by creating synergy, not fudged compromise to which no individual has total commitment. Unwarranted conflict in work and social environments may be perceived as a predictable outcome of differing personal value systems contributing to the achievement of a common goal.

The key question is – How might you learn the perspective of others, and therefore seek to rectify your blind spots?

Understanding the differences, considering the differences and integrating the differences is the starting point for developing synergy, where the result has greater value than the sum of the parts.

Unwarranted conflict, effectively managed, creates personal growth opportunities, creative decision-making and corporate renewal. Unwarranted conflict creates the opportunity to be effectively self-dependent within an inter-dependent environment.

While it is not your role as leader or manager to play the therapist, these understandings can still guide your efforts to improve the handling of conflict among those you manage. A good first step is to clearly delineate for everyone involved the structures and tools that will be employed to create a safe container for productive conflict. Because common early experiences equate conflict with a threat to survival, a commitment to safety and trust must form the foundation of all such strategies.

This is why it is so important to engage in collaborative decision-making whenever possible: people will only feel safe in the face of conflict when they know their views and concerns will be heard without judgment. The trick is to convey the understanding that everyone's ideas and input are valued, but decisions will be made with the highest good for the business in mind. This means that no one's ideas are ever belittled, mocked, or dismissed outright; rather, we can ask the person offering an idea to elaborate on why they believe their idea is good for business. It opens the way for others involved to make their own suggestions if the person in question falters in their reasoning, taking the focus off of them and returning it to the common goals that are bigger than any one person.

Such collaborative processes facilitate people in leaving their egos at the door and remaining aware of the bigger picture, thus making the best use of everyone's time and energy. It is the role of the manager to not only lay the ground rules and set the space, but to lead by example in this regard.

Meeting Everyone's Needs Through Collaboration

In an insightful contribution to the Harvard Business Review's online edition entitled <u>*Conflict Keeps Teams at the Top of their Game,*</u> Mark de Rond offers the following thought-provoking observation:

Contrary to popular belief, harmony in teams is far more likely to be the consequence — and not the cause — of performance. In fact, the best way to bond team members may well be to set them a challenge — to give them something to feel good about collectively.

In the same article, Mr. de Rond points out that conflict is most generative when it stems from a difference of opinion, rather than a personal attack:

*Conflicting opinions are important not only because they smoke out assumptions and enlarge the pool of available information, but **because they reveal what matters most to those involved.***

I bolded this last phrase because it underscores what I believe to be a core component of successful collaborative leadership strategies: the clear assurance that everyone's needs are equally valued, even if they can't always be fully met. Interestingly, I recently came across a moving example of this in a blog post by noted Conscious Parenting facilitator Karin Petersen. While this may seem unrelated, clearly it is highly relevant in light of what we know about the power of inner child work:

On July 4th I found myself negotiating with Asher about going to a friend's house. He said he didn't want to leave home, and his friend also wanted to stay home. I was hoping he would play with his friend so I could work on my computer. After some negotiating, we hit a stalemate. A few minutes later, he walked up to me and said, "It's really important to me that we stay home today." That phrase is magic. A few minutes later, we were in the car on our way to his friend's house. How did this happen, you ask?

It's the magic phrase – "This is important to me." I started asking children to use this phrase over 10 years ago as a way to communicate that they really valued something, and I use it in return. So when we are trying to figure out how to work through a conflict of interest, and as parents we often find our needs competing with our children's, it's helpful to know how much flex space there is on someone else's end. But this Fourth of July, Asher taught me something new about this phrase. I could tell, when he said it, that it was a silent request for empathy. He just wanted me to acknowledge that it was important to him, and that I am holding his needs in consideration. After he said it I reflected back to him: "Yes, I hear that it's important to you to stay home today. Tell me about that." And he did. And then he was ready to hear me. I shared my idea of going to his friend's house and simply connecting to find out what everyone wanted and needed.

He gladly hopped into the car once he felt considered. Often, we humans dog for our needs and get attached to a particular outcome, and as parents it's incredibly helpful to hear the need beyond the strategy, knowing that what our children want most is to be heard and considered. We are often not all that attached to a particular strategy, even though we may think and say we are.

Fascinating, isn't it? With adults as well as children, a simple empathic acknowledgment of someone's needs on behalf of an authority figure magically creates space for a collaborative solution to emerge.

Of course, there are times when collaborative decision-making is not possible due to constraints on time or other resources, and there are even times when it is not necessary. In such situations, a manager may be forced to act more or less unilaterally, or may choose to accommodate the wishes of others to stoke positive relations if the stakes are not particularly high. However, while these other styles of managing conflict will always have their place, only a primarily collaborative model will stimulate creativity among team members by offering them a sense of empowerment.

It is an easily observable fact that people's energy levels increase when they feel empowered, but decrease when they feel they have no say in a decision. By empowering team members to resolve conflict as collaboratively as possible, you literally make increased energy levels a part of your positive organisational culture. Since no one can be productive when their energy is low, you may as well offer healthier refreshments in place of coffee and donuts at meetings while you're at it!

Raymond and I often remind my clients that paying attention to their health must be their highest priority if they really want to reach their full potential. You'll never achieve your goals if you can't get out of bed in the morning!

Chapter 6
Get What You Want With
Relationship Intelligence

When we understand the needs that motivate our own and others' behaviour, we have no enemies. – Marshall Rosenberg

In Chapter 5, we learned that a major key to successful collaboration is the expression of empathy for what matters most to those involved. When we make this our first priority as leaders and managers, team members feel safe to relax their attachment to particular strategies for meeting their needs, because they feel assured that every effort will be made to do so.

Even when resource constraints make it impossible to fully meet the needs of every party, there will be far less conflict when people have reason to believe that their needs and viewpoints are valued. This underscores one of the fundamental goals of trust-based collaborative leadership: to create a culture in which there is an *assumption of positive intent on behalf of all parties.* That is, to ensure that no person or group perceives any other person or group as an adversary, but as teammates working toward a common goal.

Adopting this approach does not mean that we cannot allow, or even foster, a healthy sense of rivalry between individuals, but it must take place against a background of good-natured competition, not antagonism.

When people feel safe to bring their diverse viewpoints to the table without feeling personally threatened, conflict becomes a source of energy, instead of a drain on it. This provides a much greater boost to productivity than simply shutting down conflict when it arises and exhorting people to be team players. There may be no 'I' in the word 'team,' but that doesn't mean that dissenting viewpoints lack value.

Compassionate Communication At Work

Decades ago, a clinical psychologist named Dr. Marshall Rosenberg originated the powerful set of tools known as *Compassionate Communication*, or *Nonviolent Communication*, with the express purpose of creating a more peaceful world by articulating and meeting the needs behind every human word and deed. It does this by breaking all communication down into statements of feelings and needs, followed by a request for action from other parties in an effort to meet those needs. Nonviolent Communication is founded on compassionate regard for others, and the *assumption of positive intent.*

To exercise compassion at work means to be able to walk in the shoes of others. This is not always easy, and the expression of feelings within the context of what is being felt and communicated provide context that has to be managed with empathy and sensitivity.

Compassion is about respect and trust, seeing the other person as a whole. To date, the most profound reading that I have accessed in regard to compassion is in Martin Buber's book, <u>I and Thou</u>. Buber says: *The life of a human being is not passed in the sphere of transitive verbs alone. It does not exist in virtue of activities alone which have something for their object. I perceive something. I am sensible of something. I imagine something. I will something. I feel something. I think something.......This and the like together establish the realm of it. (in other words the context). But the realm of Thou has a different basis. When Thou is spoken, the speaker has no thing for his object. For where there is a thing, there is another thing. Every 'it' is bounded by others; it exists only through being bounded by others. But when Thou is spoken, there is no thing. Thou has no bounds. When Thou is spoken, the speaker has no thing; he has indeed nothing. But he takes his stand in relation.*

I find that Buber challenges me to speak and listen from no thing, also known as 'nothing.' When I listen compassionately from nothing, I open up the channel for possibilities, and as my mentor would say, I 'listen a person into existence.'

So how are you listening for possibilities? How might you listen others into existence?

In my earlier work as a **Thinking Environment** consultant as developed by Nancy Kline[8], I learned that just to listen is an act of empowerment. Listening creates empathy and compassion, listening to yourself, your body, your thoughts, listening up to others.

Nancy Kline says: *Listening is more than just not talking. It is as profound and delicate a process as entering the wood in the hope that life will go on swinging and scuttling and leaning towards the sun even with your arrival. Everything about you will have an effect on your partner's (the person being listened to) ability to keep thinking. You will want to be aware of the multitude of things you are doing and communicating while not becoming self-conscious. You will be balancing between awareness of yourself on the one hand, and an abandoned involvement in your partner's thinking on the other.*

Words are not enough for this big job. Listening at this level involves your whole body and mind. Your body will be a barometer for your partner.

I find the birth of compassion through the act of listening, and I am reminded of the tenets of Taoism, Listening and Receptivity, as outlined by Peter Reason[9]:

To be able to listen – really, wholly, passively, self effacingly listen – without presupposing, classifying, improving, controverting, evaluating, approving or disapproving, without duelling with what is being said, without rehearsing the rebuttal in advance, without free associating to portions of what is being said so that succeeding portions are not heard at all – such listening is rare. But if we can do so, says Maslow, these are the moments when we are closest to reality.

Listening to understand, listening to empower, listening to be whole and complete, listening to birth a new consciousness, listening to harmonise, listening to end the war and conflict in the inner and outer environment.

As Dr. Rosenberg's quote at the beginning of this chapter suggests, when we keep our focus on the underlying needs behind our own desires and those of others, we minimize destructive conflict while maximizing the potential for satisfaction on all sides.

The first condition that must be met for this to happen is clarity: you must be highly specific in asking for what you want, and you must foster the ability of others on your team to do the same. Lack of clarity in communication results from either a simple lack of skill, or from fear of conflict. The first issue is easily addressed with appropriate trainings, and the second will be mitigated by your efforts to create a culture of psychological safety, in which conflict is dealt with in a healthy way. When you hold your authority with clarity of intention, others feel safe and empowered to do their best work.

You will find that, when you have more clarity in your life, you have more confidence. With clarity you show up with aims, goals and intention. I have been trained by Brendon Burchard as a certified high-performance coach.

Brendon says, *The world's highest performers have remarkable clarity about who they are, how they treat others, and what life principles and practices keep them progressing and performing at their best.*

"As I have said, the first thing is to be honest with yourself. You can never have an impact on society if you have not changed yourself... Great peacemakers are all people of integrity, of honesty, but [also of] humility." — Nelson Mandela

Chapter 6

Vulnerability As Courage

Few persons are born courageous and brave. Courage is developed with consistent brave actions. All visionaries need the courage to dare to dream. Ron Howard's popular film, *Apollo 13*, dramatized the incredible events that took place from April 13-17, 1970 when a crippled spaceship was brought safely back to Earth by the courageous efforts of the NASA Team in Houston, and by the astronauts themselves.

Imagine yourself as courageous, like the brave souls depicted in this film. Remember that the original definition of 'courage' comes from the Latin word 'cor,' meaning 'heart,' and that the earliest definition was to show you are who you are by telling your story with your whole heart.

The key figure who made the Apollo rescue possible was Eugene Kranz, the flight director of the Apollo 13 mission. On that mission, the crew were faced with the danger of consuming all their oxygen and power before they were near to earth. Even if they survived re-entry, they would have had no way of controlling the plunge of their capsule back to Earth. Despite these incredibly high-stakes problems, Eugene Kranz was able to engineer a safe return for the astronauts.

Leading yourself and your business requires courage, yet you may not be achieving your full potential because of fear. Allow yourself to slowly read and reflect on the following passage from *A Return to Love*, by Marianne Williamson[10].

"Our deepest fear is not that we are inadequate... Our deepest fear is that we are powerful beyond measure. It is our light, not our darkness, that most frightens us. We ask ourselves, who am I to be brilliant, gorgeous, talented, and fabulous? Actually, who are you not to be? You are a child of God. Your playing small doesn't serve the world. There's nothing enlightened about shrinking so that other people won't feel insecure around you. We are all meant to shine, as children do. We were born to make manifest the glory of God that is within us. It's not just in some of us; it's in everyone. And as we let our own light shine, we unconsciously give other people permission to do the same. As we're liberated from our own fear, our presence automatically liberates others."

You are more likely to demonstrate your courage if you are able to transcend fear. Fear's purpose is to signal to you that an issue is important. Yet if you become paralysed by fear, you will procrastinate and take no action. Unchecked fear then becomes disabling, because excessive fear closes down your solar plexus, which is a close network of nerves with connecting tissue at the bottom of your rib cage. The solar plexus is sometimes referred to as the sun of the body, and if this 'sun' is closed down in you, you will not shine.

The first step in your journey to leadership starts with courage. The voice of your experience can be a catalyst and inspiration to others. I teach my clients the value of stories. Story as a tool, not only helps you to influence others, it also helps you to self-govern, says Annette Simmons [11] Storytelling transports people to different points of view so that they can reinterpret or reframe what your facts mean to them.

I have illustrated the courage of Eugene Kranz, and I have presented questions for you to reflect upon your acts of courage. I encourage you to use your stories to illustrate leading with courage and in so doing focus on:

- Control
- Overview
- Understanding
- Resilience
- Accountable
- Global
- Engaged

Control your fears and have compassion for yourself and for others. Control of your fears often leads you to do what is right. Courage, compassion and wisdom are closely related. In regard to courage, wisdom is like food to you when you are starving. When you know that you are going in the right direction, you are able to face every obstacle with supreme confidence that your difficulties can be overcome.

Another story that exemplifies courage relates to Malala Yousafzai. She was shot in the head on a school bus by Taliban gunmen October 2012 because of her campaign for girls' rights to education. Malala has been credited with bringing the issue of women's education to global attention. A quarter of young women around the world have not completed primary school. Speaking on her 16th birthday in July 2013, Malala, was wearing a pink shawl that belonged to assassinated Pakistan leader Benazir Bhutto. Malala is a winner of the Nobel Peace Prize, and all efforts to silence her have failed. In her courageous address to the United Nations, she said: *"I am here to speak up for the right of education of every child."*

Malala received several standing ovations during her address on Friday, 12 July 2013 to the United Nations (UN). Malala told the UN on that the Taliban's attack had only made her more resolute. She said, *"The terrorists thought that they would change my aims and stop my ambitions, but nothing changed in my life, except this: weakness, fear and hopelessness died. Strength, power and courage were born."*

She uttered: *"I want education for the sons and daughters of the Taliban and all the terrorists and extremists... The extremists were, and they are, afraid of books and pens... They are afraid of women. I am fighting for the rights of women because they are the ones who suffer the most."*

Leading with courage requires an overview of the whole situation. Do you know where the calculated risks are? What is your understanding of the issues? How resilient are you? When did you shine with your resilience? What are the valuable lessons from your setbacks? How accountable are you? Responsibility is your belief that you are in charge of your own actions. What are the global and universal stories that reflect your story? How engaged and connected are you?

In bringing the Apollo 13 astronauts safely back to Earth, Kranz's courage was not a product of blind faith. Rather, it was the personification of trained confidence. He knew that he had a good team in place, and he believed with his whole heart that the solutions could be found. He reminded his staff that *"once you think of surrendering... That is the path that you will take. As soon as you start to think that way, you have lost... the mental sharpness, the mental edge that is going to take the survival situation and take it to a successful conclusion."*

Many spiritual teachings maintain that, while we may not always get what we want in life, we do always get what we need. The trick, then, is to close the gap between what we want, and what we need. As a leader, this requires of you the ability to trust that when you articulate your needs and your vision for getting them met, the Universe will deliver a solution, *even if it does not look how you expect.*

Some people might perceive this relinquishment of control as weakness, but the work of pioneering social researcher Brené Brown has shown that *true vulnerability is perceived as courage.* In her two wildly popular TED talks, she shares what she has learned about the power of vulnerability to create what she calls a 'wholehearted life.'

Just as true courage correlates strongly with vulnerability, true power correlates strongly with humility.

U.S. President Harry S. Truman said *"it is amazing what you can accomplish if you don't care who gets the credit,"* and this attitude is at the heart of effective collaborative leadership. Leaders get much of the credit when things go well, and much of the blame when they don't, but humility allows you to extract maximum learning out of either situation.

Your efforts at non-attachment will pay off in your ability to view each situation with neutrality, which is always the most powerful place from which to make decisions.

Another advantage of having the courage to let go of being right is that it allows the Law of Attraction to bring you solutions in ways that your mind would never have been able to anticipate. When we become fixated on a certain outcome, we limit what is possible, but there is a difference between fixation and intention. Fixation indicates an excessively narrow focus and attachment to particular scenarios.

Many of us think that intention is about getting things done, but it is at least as much about being as it is about doing. In its higher manifestations, intention is about invoking the highest and best outcome for all involved, then listening for inner guidance as to what actions to take to bring this about. Your clear *intention*, directed by your full *attention*, is what creates results, when the actions you take align with the guidance of your intuition. Albert Einstein famously said, *If I had an hour to solve a problem, I'd spend 55 minutes thinking about the problem, and 5 minutes thinking about solutions.*

Another way of saying this is that, if you don't ask the right questions, every answer will seem wrong. If you are not getting what you want, this is simply a signal from the universe to step back, get quiet, and ask better questions. We can choose at any point to let go of attachment and invite a new perspective. This is one of the most vital skills that a good coach contributes to his or her clients: the ability to ask better questions, for the purpose of revealing new avenues of possibility.

The Cornerstone of a Culture of Excellence

As a leader, the more you experience being coached, the better-equipped you will be to facilitate collaborative decision-making among your team members. The popularity of executive coaching has exploded in part because managers have realised that effective coaching has many important skills in common with effective leadership: skilful communication, accountability, empathy, and the ability to zero in on the right line of questioning. The more you practice being a client, the better you will become at playing the role of coach for the people you manage in an inspiring and productive way.

"Differences are not intended to separate, to alienate. We are different precisely in order to realize our need of one another."
— *Desmond Tutu*

As you become more comfortable with collaborative leadership strategies, you may find yourself becoming more aware of how to make your gain other people's gain as well. When you've established a culture of collaboration, it becomes a simple matter to frame your victories as other people's victories. You'll automatically begin to consider what others have to gain, and you can use these benefits as selling points when asking others to help you get what you want. Not only is this a constructive way to manage conflict, if your achievement affects others' lives positively, they will be more likely to help you in the future.

This is a core truth about relationships: that they thrive on respect, integrity, clarity, and above all, *consistency*. Dr. Martyn Newman says, *as a leader, it is your responsibility to create expectations and protocols founded on trust, fairness, and clear communication.* In doing so, you generate emotional capital with your team that is just as valuable as money when it comes to getting what you want.

At this stage, we need to address one of the fundamental factors that will strongly influence your ability to successfully implement these strategies with your teams. Here it is: as a leader or manager, you stand the best chance of getting what you want when each team member has explicitly agreed to be held to high standards. That is, you cannot push someone to grow past their comfort zones without their express permission. As anyone with significant management experience knows, one bad apple really can spoil the barrel. That is why, to the greatest extent possible, you want to avoid hiring individuals who lack the humility and /or self-esteem to work well collaboratively. For this reason, the creation of a culture of excellence must begin with the hiring process; you must clearly inform all prospective employees that they will be pushed to excel if they agree to work for you.

Warren Buffet puts it this way:

Somebody once said that in looking for people to hire, you look for three qualities: integrity, intelligence, and energy. And if you don't have the first, the other two will kill you.

Along the same lines, he also said that *"it takes 20 years to build a reputation, and five minutes to ruin it. If you think about that, you'll do things differently."* The most valuable additions to your team are people whose reputations and behaviour demonstrate a high level of commitment to integrity. When you make it your business to hire only such people whenever possible, you improve the likelihood that you will be able to get what you want with a collaborative leadership style. These people have the self-confidence to appreciate being pushed, and your efforts to walk the talk will not go unnoticed by them. When your employees understand that they are working with you, not only for you, it's easier to get what you want in a way that works for all.

[8] Nancy Kline, More Time to Think: A Way of Being In The World. Kingfisher Publishing. England 2009

[9] Peter Reason and John Rowan, Human Inquiry: A Sourcebook of New Paradigm Research p. 89. Wiley 1981

[10] Marianne Williamson, A Course in Miracles, Foundation for Inner Peace

[11] Annette Simmons, Whoever Tells the Best Story Wins: How To Use Your Own Stories to Communicate with Power and Impact. American Management Association 2007. ISBN-13 978-0-8144-0914-5

Chapter 7
Remember to Enjoy the Journey

"Happiness is not a goal, it's a by-product of a life well lived."
— *Eleanor Roosevelt*

In this chapter I want you to understand that the more you are in relationship with who you are and doing what you love, the more your prosperity will flow. It is becoming more and more apparent that humanity is waking up; we are beginning to understand the truth of Ralph Waldo Emerson's adage that *'life is a journey, not a destination.'*

Eleanor Roosevelt and many other visionaries understood intuitively that the present moment is all we ever have, and it is our everyday choices about how to respond to life that determine the happiness available to us.

When you study the lives of such visionaries across cultures and time periods, there is a common thread that ties them all together: every one of them, without exception, has loved what they did and been driven by a vision whose clarity never wavered. Passion arises from the heart, and vision arises from the soul.

Chapter 7

Passion is a personal experience. When you begin to do what you love, engaging with the activities and pursuits that make your heart sing, you will find your life being pulled in directions that you may not even begin to imagine. You will discover an irresistible magic when you open your heart to your passion, to what you love and care about.

So often, we allow ourselves to get bogged down with the "how," saying to ourselves: how will I find the money? How will I master the skill? How will I make a success of this at this stage of my life?

But if there's one thing I have learned, it's that the important thing is not the 'how,' it is the 'why.' The tapestry of your life is stitched together by a unifying, universal knowledge that is manifested from joy. Think about your conception from the orgasm of your parents. What are your true passions?

The pursuit of your passion is the thread that weaves the various segments of your life into a cohesive whole. If you are not pursuing your passions, then you are not going to be happy for long, and you are not going to sustain progress for very long either.

I am talking about passion here as what you love, not as lust. Remember that what you love and God's love for you are two sides of the same coin. You are living in a universe that is designed to deliver the greatest possible joy, the greatest possible experience of fulfilment, when you are ready and open to receive it.

Did you know that a survey of 100 of the most influential and financially successful people revealed that they have one thing in common? Can you guess what the one thing it is?

The answer is, they all say that they enjoy their lives.

The whole purpose of life is to enjoy it. When you are not enjoying life, you have stepped out of God's flow, and you are missing your passion and your purpose.

If you are wondering why it is so important to enjoy life and enjoy what you are doing, think about the people on this planet past and present have made the greatest contribution: every one of them, without exception, has loved what they did.

Now think of the people whom you know to be truly happy: what are the characteristics that are common to them?

Do they love what they are doing in their lives? Maybe there are some of parts of their lives that are challenging but, when it comes right down to it, they love their lives. They love what they spend their days doing, and the people with whom they spend their time.

"Passion is the inner fire that propels you forward through all the combination of love for what you are doing, and the inner sense of purpose that comes from connecting to your deepest passions. Enjoyment arises from the combination of love and purposefulness."
- Janet Bray Attwood and Chris Atwood, co-creators of The Passion Test

Chapter 7

"God has given each of us our marching orders. Our purpose here on earth is to find those orders and carry them out. Those orders acknowledge our special gifts."
- Soren Kierkeegaard

When you are passionate about the vision that guides your steps, taking those steps doesn't feel like a struggle. If that passion and vision are strong enough, they will hold even when challenges arise, and you will easily find ways to overcome those challenges.

Obstacles may slow you down, but they will not stop you, though you may pause a moment to reflect. If, upon reflection, you determine that a change in direction is called for, you will simply change your tack and move on. Relationships, like all aspects of life, are about flow. They are most productive when the people involved can strike an ideal balance between giving and receiving, for this is the crux of all relationships. Like a river coursing down a mountain, the flow of energy in a relationship usually follows the path of least resistance, instinctively avoiding obstacles and even wearing them down slowly over time, as trust is established. Some rivers flow smoothly, and others roil with rapids and whirlpools but, in either case, the water is flowing.

So here's the question: How might I encourage you to smooth the way?

Beyond the strategies, tools, and insights that I have covered so far, how might you choose to be in order to turn a narrow, rocky canyon into a wide and sandy delta?

It may surprise you to learn that one of the most powerful ways that we may be is to infuse all of our relationships with greater ease, *to be at ease and to enjoy our own journey.* Yet it is only surprising until you remember that, like every other aspect of life, relationships are governed by the universal Law of Attraction. And what is the one common denominator that links all of your relationships together? *The answer is you – it is the vibrations you put out that determine what someone else can bring to their relationship with you.* Author and speaker Dr. Joe Vitale, like Raymond, is a contributor to the film <u>The Secret.</u> He puts it this way:

"It's really important that you feel good. Because this feeling good is what goes out as a signal into the universe and starts to attract more of itself to you. So the more you can feel good, the more you will attract the things that help you feel good, and that will keep bringing you up higher and higher."

Positivity Rules

Like others who have used their knowledge of the Law of Attraction to create highly fulfilling lives, Dr. Vitale teaches that positive emotion is the best indicator that you have aligned yourself with the flow of the Universe. Negative emotion is meant only to serve as an indication that you have somehow diverged from this flow in thought, word or deed. Often when we hear teachers like Dr. Vitale explain these principles, it sounds almost too simplistic, and we are left wondering why the Law of Attraction seems to work so well for them, but yields much less dramatic results for so many others.

There is no question that some people do seem to obtain results more quickly than others, and the reason for this is a topic for another book. However, what Raymond and I have both noticed in my work as a coach and in my own life is that, as with so many other things, implementing the Law of Attraction successfully takes *practice*. And it's not simply a matter of coming up with affirmations that we repeat endlessly in the hopes that this will be enough to change our point of attraction; to really achieve this, we must undertake the courageous work of shining light into the shadows of our subconscious, where the wounded parts of our inner child cower.

Only when we make the unconscious, conscious do we become free to release our resistance to life, instead of struggling against it. This is the best way I know of to return our lives, and all the relationships they contain, to a state of flow and balance.

Prisons Are of Our Own Making

"As I walked out the door toward the gate that would lead to my freedom, I knew if I didn't leave my bitterness and hatred behind, I'd still be in prison." – Nelson Mandela

We are so used to labelling things as 'right' or 'wrong,' as 'good' or 'bad,' and often we are trained from an early age to place a high value on being right. However, it is very important that we question these beliefs, for the following reason: often in life, obstacles arise to show us where we are holding onto beliefs and concepts that are no longer true for us, and for this reason we will suffer if we are not open to letting go of our most cherished ideas about ourselves, others, and the world.

In Chapter 3, I used the example of Holocaust survivor Alice Herz Sommer to illustrate the power of optimism. Yet I believe that Alice's power went beyond a mere positive outlook: her life was an illustration of what happens when a person simply refuses every temptation the world offers them to drop their vibration. War came, and incarceration came, her family was killed and almost every vestige of happiness banished from her life; yet while she may have momentarily grieved her circumstances, Alice never let them take away her power to choose.

She simply decided that she would be happy no matter what, because she understood – indeed, her mother had taught her from an early age – that *no one can take away your happiness unless you let them,* no matter what they do to you, for our power to choose makes it so.

The same goes for all life circumstances, even if we have no one to blame for them but God; they only have as much power over us as we give them. Enjoying the journey, then, is not simply a luxury that some have and some don't; it is a choice you can make at any time, and that you *must* make if you wish to lead a fulfilling life, regardless of circumstances.

When we really take this in, it quickly becomes apparent what a tall order it is for most of us to choose to be happy no matter what. Our subconscious minds are so sure that victimhood is real, that there are times when the world is just out to get us. Those less-conscious parts of us are so reluctant to admit they've been lying to themselves all this time, choosing to play the victim instead of seeking to expand in love and awareness.

Think about it, though: if Alice Herz Sommers does not view herself as a victim, then what excuse does any of us have to do so? From her story of the triumph of love and awareness over cruelty and ignorance, we learn that nothing has the power to bring us down unless we let it. Like a loving parent comforting an ashamed or frightened child, it is the job of our conscious awareness to nurture the subconscious back towards a feeling of safety, reminding it that it is always loved no matter what it says or does. The last thing we should do is take its antics personally, as good parents well know!

Mindfulness, Awareness, Gratitude

If we are to transcend the matrix of consciousness that keeps too many of us trapped in the belief that we are powerless, we must be willing to slowly, gently, begin to confront the places where we give away our power. Mindfulness is a wonderful tool for this, as it teaches us to simply return our awareness to each moment as it unfolds, noticing where our minds add their own layers of interpretation.

Gratitude is another powerful tool – few things are more effective to raise your vibration quickly. Finally, it is extremely helpful to set a deliberate intention at the beginning of each day, because this activates the Law of

Attraction on your behalf. It takes some time to re-train our brains from victimhood to power, but with discipline and the loving support of helpers seen and unseen, it will happen. All that is required is patience, compassion, and the ability to ask for and receive help. As I discussed earlier, vulnerability is not weakness, but the gateway to true power.

One of the best ways to become more mindful is to tie this awareness practice in with particular aspects of your daily routine. In my opinion, the most powerful time to practice mindfulness, gratitude, or setting an intention for your day is first thing in the morning.

This is because the intention that we begin our day with sets the tone for the rest of our day; you can create anxiety and distraction by checking your email and voicemail first thing, or you can create focus and calm by taking a few moments to breathe deeply, meditate, or practice yoga or other techniques for energy management and raising consciousness.

When you realise that your decision to enjoy the journey is the very thing that makes it more enjoyable, your relationships will adjust to reflect this choice, and you will be well on your way to a happier and more productive life.

Chapter 8
Relationships Are About Learning

The greatest glory in living lies not in never falling, but in rising every time we fall. — *Nelson Mandela*

In the last chapter, I touched on the idea that relationships are one of the universe's favourite ways to draw our attention to areas of growth and learning. Here is the core: no matter what our egos may want or think they need, what our spirits are interested in is growth. It is our spirits that choose to incarnate, that wish to experience this plane of reality for the purpose of growth and learning.

This part of us never forgets that it is a choice, and the more we can recognise this and surrender the need for control, the easier our life journey can be. Indeed, this is the way to get maximum fulfilment out of life, even if it is sometimes scary. It requires faith in a benevolent universe and an ability to believe in oneself, both of which simply come with practice.

The degree to which we allow learning experiences to affect us emotionally is up to us, yet this is a topic that constitutes an area of learning by itself for most of us.

Sometimes at first, we are surprised to learn just how powerful we are, but once we do, the freedom that comes with taking responsibility for our learning becomes exhilarating.

There is greatness within you. Reflect on the following:

Each of us is great in so far as we perceive and act on the infinite possibilities which lie undiscovered and unrecognized about us.
- James Harvey Robinson

What If You Chose This Life?

A good coach can be an invaluable ally as you undertake this journey, because a coach is able to support you in pushing past the limits of your current perceptions to reveal new and exciting vistas of possibility. A common tool used by coaches to this end is prompts for reflective journaling. Here is one that Raymond likes to assign his clients to help them recognize and exercise their power of choice:

Just for fun, suppose that you chose this life. Suppose that, before you were born, you had a chat with God, and God said to you, 'what do you want to learn this lifetime?' Suppose that you and God then mapped out major points in your life experience, with plenty of room built in for you to exercise your free will. Re-imagine your entire life as if you had deliberately chosen it, as if this mortal life were only a lesson plan. Imagine that the events of your life have come in answer to a request that you made for guidance from God. Be open to the possibility that, even if your life has been difficult, maybe these experiences have served to teach you something that you asked to learn about — they're answers to your requests. The thing you resist persists; remember that you can only release the pattern once you've learned the lesson.

With this insight, we encounter the possibility that the very purpose of relationships is to help us to learn life's lessons, thereby creating space for our consciousness to evolve into higher vibrational frequencies.

Perhaps we are here to participate with others in a graceful dance of mutual growth that moves all into higher states of consciousness. As I have discussed, however, this can only happen if we choose it, and the only choices that you have power over are your own. This is why we must do our best to appreciate the lessons that people bring us without trying to change others beyond agreed-upon boundaries.

This means that, when it becomes clear that someone who works for you is unwilling or unable to grow with you and the rest of the company, you know the time has come to let that person go.

At such times, you must remember that fulfilling spiritual contracts is not the same thing as pleasing people's egos, and you must be prepared for the possibility that your role in someone's learning will cause them to dislike you. This is par for the course in the lives of most human beings, and must not be taken personally.

Chapter 8

Stay In Your Business to Stay Out of Stress

Do I know what's right for me? That is my only business. Let me work with that before I try to solve problems for you. – Byron Katie, Loving What Is

On the subject of not taking things personally, there is a spiritual teacher named Byron Katie[12] who has helped thousands of people take this idea to a new level with a remarkably straightforward process known simply as 'The Work.'

The Work is designed to help individuals get at what is really true for them, underneath the false concepts that they may have subconsciously chosen to believe. Her books are well worth reading, as they convey very clearly just how powerful this form of inquiry is. One of the many valuable insights she offers is the idea that all human beings share the same kinds of misperceptions, and *we therefore should not take our own limitations personally.* Without this insight, we run the risk of becoming extremely attached to our way being right, resulting in others perceiving us as arrogant and resisting our attempts to influence them.

Power struggles stem from individuals attempting to force their ideas on each other in this way, each clinging so doggedly to their own viewpoint that they are unable to perceive solutions that may be amenable to both. When we begin to let this go, however, we gain the ability to disengage from power struggles and uncover solutions that can move everyone forward. Not only is this a more effective way to work with others, it is also much less stressful.

The Work demonstrates very clearly that stress always results from a dissonance between what is really true and the story we tell ourselves about reality. In her book, Byron Katie highlights the importance of staying in your own business to reduce the stress that comes from believing we are separate from others.

The following passage from the book elaborates on what this means:

I can find only three kinds of business in the universe: mine, yours, and God's. Much of our stress comes from mentally living out of our business. When I think, "You need to get a job, I want you to be happy, you should be on time, you need to take better care of yourself," I am in your business. When I'm worried about earthquakes, floods, war, or when I will die, I am in God's business. If I am mentally in your business or in God's business, the effect is separation.

I believe that regularly practicing the type of inquiry outlined in the Work, as well as studying compassionate communication and inspirational leadership, can deeply transform your experience of all your relationships. The more you understand what true power is, the more you become able to stay in your business and let go of being right, and the more others will be inspired to follow your example. This is because, subconsciously, they will realize that you have found an inner freedom, and they will want that for themselves. Inspirational leadership can be powerful indeed, but it does require that you walk your talk.

Forgiveness is Vital to Learning

Resentment is like drinking poison and then hoping it will kill your enemies. — Nelson Mandela

Relationships that challenge our pre-conceived ideas and prejudices can lead us to freedom, but only when we choose to learn their lessons. Paradoxically, sometimes we cannot make this choice until we let go of what it took to arrive at it, because a lack of forgiveness towards ourselves or towards others prevents us from moving forward.

The former South African leader Nelson Mandela's 'Long Walk to Freedom' was successful in large part because he understood this. He led his nation through an intense process of truth and reconciliation, knowing that it was the only way to achieve lasting peace between his people's former oppressors, and those they had oppressed.

God doesn't judge anyone's choices, and we won't either when we realise that karma is real. By this I don't only mean that people who commit evil deeds will suffer the same fate as their victims in some future incarnation, although I believe that this may be the case.

What I am implying is that, often without realising it, such perpetrators are already suffering the worst possible fate in present time: separation from God. For this reason, in a very real sense there is no point in punishing someone who has done wrong, for their unethical actions simply serve as proof that they are already suffering. We might instead explain to them why what they did was wrong and engage them in a process of healing, even if we have to lock them away for a while to prevent them from causing more harm. With time and healing, the victims may even begin to feel compassion for the perpetrators, knowing that they themselves are simply further down the path of growth than those who sinned against them. We all re-unite with Source eventually, it is just a question of when. Since our own choices are the only ones we can control, we may as well stop 'drinking the poison' and do what we can to cultivate forgiveness. When we do, we become a beacon for those who are still trapped in suffering.

The Power of Responsibility

Dr Ihaleakala Hew Len[13] demonstrated the healing power of claiming 100 percent responsibility for his clients' problems when he used Ho'oponopono, an ancient Hawaiian clearing technique now updated and modified to four simple phrases. Relying just on this simple technique and his stance that his role was to assume full responsibility for having created the patients' problems in the first place, Dr Len healed all the patients within the medical ward of a prison.

Morrnah Naamaku Simeona, the creator of Self I-Dentity Ho'oponopono and a Living Treasure of the State of Hawaii, had this to say about the clearing process, *"Ho'oponopono is a profound gift that allows one to develop a working relationship with the Divinity within and learn to ask that in each moment, our errors in thought, word, deed or action be cleansed. The process is essentially about freedom, complete freedom from the past."* [14]

When using Ho'oponopono approach, a process of repentance, forgiveness, and transmutation, a therapist is able to have erroneous thoughts, within himself and within the client, transmuted into perfect thoughts of LOVE. As erroneous thoughts are replaced by loving thoughts in the therapist and in his family, relatives and ancestors, they too are replaced in the client and in her family, relatives and ancestors. Ho'oponopono allows the therapist to work directly with the Original Source who can transmute erroneous thoughts into LOVE.

Following this form of healing, the therapist first takes his I-Dentity, his mind, and connects it up to the Original Source, what others call LOVE or GOD. With the connection in place, the therapist then appeals to LOVE to correct the erroneous thoughts within him that are actualising the problem, firstly for himself, and secondly, for the client. The appeal is a process of repentance and forgiveness on the part of the therapist, who is implicitly saying, "I am sorry for the erroneous thoughts within me that have caused the problem for the client; please forgive me." In response to the repentance and forgiveness appeal of the therapist, LOVE begins the mystical process of transmuting the erroneous thoughts.

In this spiritual correction process, LOVE first neutralizes the erroneous emotions that have caused the problem, be they resentment, fear, anger, blame or confusion. In the next step, LOVE then releases the neutralized energies from the thoughts, leaving them in a state of void, of emptiness, of true freedom.

LOVE then fills the newly emptied space with Itself. The result? The therapist is renewed, restored in LOVE. As the therapist is renewed so is the client and all involved in the problem. Where there was despair in the client, there is now LOVE. Where there was darkness in her soul, there is now the healing light of LOVE.

The wonder of Ho'oponopono is that you get to meet yourself anew in each moment, and you get to appreciate more and more with each application the process of renewing the miracle of LOVE.

I operate my life and my relationships according to the following insights:

1. The Physical Universe is actualized of my thoughts.
2. If my thoughts are cancerous, they create a cancerous physical reality.
3. If my thoughts are perfect, they create a physical reality brimming with LOVE.
4. I am 100 percent responsible for creating my physical universe the way it is.
5. I am 100 responsible for correcting the cancerous thoughts that create a diseased reality.
6. There is no such thing as out there. Everything exists as a thought in my mind.

It is important to note that we commonly use blame to avoid taking responsibility. We always need to remember that with any situation we have choices, namely:

(1) Acceptance – metaphysical – there is ... good in this. Accept that there are many perspectives rather than react. See the context – change the context and the possibility.

2) Fight back – Anger – failure to see the difference – Failure to look beyond the obvious. Implicit assumptions.

Which of the two is more empowering? Which will you choose in any relationship or situation?

Gratitude is the Elixir of Life

Gratitude unlocks the fullness of life. It turns what we have into enough, and more. It turns denial into acceptance, chaos into order, confusion into clarity. It can turn a meal into a feast, a house into a home, a stranger into a friend. Gratitude makes sense of our past, brings peace for today, and creates a vision for tomorrow. – Melody Beattie

Once we understand that we are here to grow, we can be grateful for the myriad opportunities that life gives us to choose expansion. As the quote above makes clear, gratitude is the key that unlocks the door to a more fulfilling life on every level. When you make gratitude a way of life, you begin to recognize that, as Alice Herz Sommer puts it, 'everything is a present.'

Each moment, each opportunity to choose is a gift from the universe custom-built to help you grow in precisely the ways you have asked to grow. When you know this, the journey becomes joyful beyond imagining, and you stop caring whether or not you ever 'arrive.' When you truly understand that the purpose of life is to enjoy the journey, all things become possible.

There are so many ways to begin to practice gratitude. One of the simplest is to fill a page in a medium-sized notebook each day with things that you are grateful for, always trying to uncover new things to be grateful for. You can also make it a point to think only about things you are grateful for as you walk from your car or bus stop to your office, or any other time you have a few minutes to walk; this is a great way to start your morning. Raymond practices gratitude each time he gets in his car, appreciating how comfortably and efficiently it conveys him from place to place. Personally, I practice gratitude each night prior to going to sleep with the Ohm Meditation. Breathing in, I clear the channel between my root chakra and my brow chakra with the sound of Ohm, giving gratitude for breath, for life, and for all that I am.

Eventually, after you have been practicing gratitude for a while, you will find yourself becoming more and more constantly aware of the incredible abundance that is inherent in the world, if only we can notice it. The more this awareness grows in you, the less susceptible you become to fear or worry of any kind, knowing that every problem has a solution and we are never given more than we can handle. This is indeed a powerful place to stand, for it puts you in a position to become aware of right action at all times. I consciously choose as often as possible, to remind myself of right thoughts, right words, right action and right direction.

Then I find that I can lead with humility and integrity, knowing that none of us is better or worse than anyone else, but we all have the potential for greatness.

Fifteen years ago, on my first visit to South Africa and the townships, I became aware of the circumstances of people's lives, and I made a vow to myself that, no matter what, I would never again focus on what I lacked but instead would be grateful for all that I am, all that is coming to me and all that will be. Reflecting on the point in time when I met Raymond to give birth to this book, I realised that this was also the exact time when I met two other people who stand to change my life forever. Seeing these blessings, I give gratitude for all that is mine, all that I am and all that is coming to me with love and integrity.

Consider Ho'oponopono as a combined way to practice forgiveness and gratitude. As with all clearing tools given in the Ho'oponopono process, embedded within each sentence is the claiming of the responsibility for the clearing when you say:

> *I am sorry*
> *Please forgive me*
> *I love you*
> *Thank you*

All you need to do is to have the thought, that *I love you to allow love to transmute the clearing.* You don't even have to have the feeling of I love you. I know that by holding the thought of *I love you,* as previously mentioned, love will transmute the energy, clearing will occur, so that what is right and perfect will flow.

Alan Cohen, in his book <u>*Enough Already: The Power of Radical Contentment*</u>[15], commented on the big picture as follows:

All upset is the result of assuming that you know how life should be. You try to cram people and events into your model, and they do not fit; you get disappointed, frustrated and angry. But your idea of how life should be is just that – your idea. Usually your perception is authored by the ego, which sees only the tiniest piece of the picture, coloured by fear, and begets non-productive results. When you fight to swim upstream while your good lives downstream, you wear yourself down and get nowhere.

I ask spiritual teacher Ram Dass, "is it a good idea to pray for a particular result?"

He answered, "if you could be aware of all the ways the result would affect your life and the lives of everyone it touches, certainly. But no human being has the overview to know how things should turn out."

I believe that one of the most beautiful experiences within human existence is the gift of relationships. Within relationships lies the possibility of learning to give and receive love to myself and others.

In relationship, we are drawn to express higher level of consciousness, to expand our awareness of our connection to the Source from whence the wholeness of creation sprang. It is important to always bear in mind that in any relationship, the other person is a mirror of you. How do you explore presence within your interactions? How easily do you permit another individual to enter your personal space and offer unconditional love to you? How openly do you receive unconditional love? Do you question the support or praise that you receive from others? Whatever the level of compassionate relationship that challenges you, the time to transform it is now.

[12] Byron Katie, Loving What Is: Four Questions That Can Change Your Life. Harmony Books 2002

[13] Dr Ihaleakala Hew Len, cited in Zero Limits: The Secret Hawaiian System for Wealth, Health, Peace and More. Joe Vitale and Ihaleakala Hew Len p. 5-8. Wiley & Sons 2007

[14] ibid

[15] Alan Cohen, Enough Already: The Power of Radical Contentment. Hay House 2012

Conclusion
Why This Book Was Written

Raymond and I have written this book to empower you to take your life to the next level by honing your relationship skills. We believe that, when you put the wisdom I share here to the test, you will find yourself able to engage in both personal and professional relationships from a place of greater power and freedom. Not only will this feel great to you, but those you encounter will benefit as well, in a ripple effect that grows over time.

When we have the necessary skills, insights, and commitment level, relationships of all kinds become a source of numerous invaluable gifts. They allow us to become more flexible and adaptable, and to develop self-control, assertiveness and resilience, among other qualities. This is because, inevitably, relationships serve to hold up a mirror to our own beliefs and choices. We sometimes dread this aspect of relationship, but when we work to cultivate compassion and self-love, the mirror that others hold up for us will be much less harsh. This is why healing the inner child is the foundation on which all breakthroughs in emotional and relationship intelligence are built.

There is one final nugget of wisdom that I wish to leave you with as you prepare to embrace relationship more deeply than ever before. Here it is:

I believe that it is not correct to understand the Golden Rule as a commandment, as is suggested by the phrase, *do unto others as you would have them do unto you.* This implies a moral guideline that one is free to follow or not, but I believe that the biblical authors of those words were actually trying to make a statement about karmic law. With this in mind, a better translation might be, *as you do to others, you do to yourself.*

This makes it clear that there's no opting out of this one: you get what you put out into the world, no exceptions. The following excerpt from *A Course In Miracles* makes this point clearly:

When you meet anyone, remember it is a holy encounter. As you see him, you see yourself. As you treat her, you will treat yourself. As you think of him, you will think of yourself. Never forget this, for in him you will find yourself or lose yourself.

We hope that, in some small way, this book has helped you learn how to find yourself in others, instead of losing yourself in the drama that relationships sometimes bring. Our experience as coaches and organisational consultants has shown us over and over again that, when people increase their emotional intelligence and relationship skills, every aspect of their lives and work improves. We enjoy helping others to do this through writing, speaking, and coaching, and we always love to hear from those who have achieved results with the methods and practices I advocate.

We know they work, because we have seen them work for hundreds of people with a diverse range of interests, aptitudes, and personalities. However, what each of these people had in common was a high level of commitment, and a willingness to question deep-seated beliefs.

My coach brought the following quote on commitment to my consciousness and I would like you to bear the quote in mind:

Until one is committed there is always hesitancy, ineffectiveness and the chance to draw back. However, as soon as one definitely commits oneself, then and only then providence moves also. All manner of unforeseen material assistance and meetings and chance happening arise in one's favour that no one could have dreamt possible. Simply put, whatever you can dream, you can do, begin it immediately because boldness has genius, power and magic in it.
Johann Wolfgang von Goethe

You will find that, in applying your success principles, action must take first priority. You may have a vision and a dream, but until you take the first step, nothing will come of it.

Vision without action is merely a dream
Action without vision just passes the time
Vision with action can change the world
- Joel A Barker

For those who work as coaches, there is nothing more satisfying than being able to facilitate individuals in the discovery of their own inner light and resources. There is no greater joy than to learn that you already carry everything you need within, except perhaps the joy of witnessing another in this discovery. Coaching is all about empowerment, and empowerment feels good!

Power can be taken, but not given. The process of stepping into, and taking your power is empowerment.

As spiritual beings having a human experience we have the innate ability to redefine what it is to be human. So remember your true essence: Love, peace and joy. Be conscious of your Divine essence: Gratitude, appreciation, giver, worthy, lovable and completely whole.

- Be aware of your pure feelings
- Trace the feelings to the origin – where did that come from?
- Present time - shed light on it in the present time
- Make a conscious choice, I am worthy, lovable, whole and divine – take action to be lovable, whole and divine

I am the source of my experience – not the context – and I choose how I respond.

Grace is a higher power, a force of love working on your behalf. Grace supports you with Spiritual Confidence. I am still developing patience, so I invite you to reflect and be conscious as you walk the journey of life:

"Allow yourself to understand that the relaxation you experience when you "Go with the Flow" is not giving up control, it is "Taking Control." It is just that the natural control you already contain doesn't meet with resistance." [16]

"The only reason that you create impatience is because you think you need patience -- and you don't. If you are enjoying every single moment of your life because you know every single moment of your life is there for a reason, then you won't be waiting for something better to come along. And when you are not waiting for something better to come along, you don't need to be patient." [17]

- Approve of yourself.
- You will never need others to approve you.
- Your energy and your attitude is more than anything.

In conclusion, I leave you with Bashar's[18] basic message:

- You are a non-physical consciousness that is experiencing physical reality.
- You were created in the image of The Creator, your essential essence is unconditional love and the experience of ecstasy is your birthright.
- You are here on Earth at this time because you chose to be.
- The highest purpose of your life is to be yourself to the best of your ability and live each moment as fully as possible.
- You always have free will and the freedom to choose.
- Anything you can imagine is possible for you to experience.

- You attract your life experiences through the interaction of your strongest beliefs, emotions and actions.
- Excitement is the physical translation of the vibrational resonance that is your true, core natural being. Follow your excitement!
- You are naturally abundant and your choices are always supported by Creation.

If you would like to take this work even deeper, I am available to support you individually and organisationally, and would be honoured to serve you in this way. It's my joy to serve as guide as well as fellow traveller on this journey called life.

Keep in touch with me at www.Neslyn.com

[16] Eldon Taylor, What Does This Mean: Exploring Mind, Meaning and Mysteries. Hay House 2010

[17] Bashar is a multi-dimensional extra-terrestrial being who speaks through channel Darryl Anka from what we perceive as the future. Bashar explores a wide range of subjects with great insight, humour and a profound understanding of how reality creation occurs

[18] ibid

Made in the USA
Charleston, SC
29 May 2016